"I wouldn't have guessed that I ha
League Baseball coach, but Billie Ja
As soon as I read her counsel to choose 'activities that are God glorifying not
schedule stuffers,' I knew she was speaking my language. In practical and
genuine ways, *Making Room* offers us the tools we need to leave space for God
to work in our lives and through our lives. A book to which I'll no doubt need to
return often."

—Cynthia Ruchti, author of *A Fragile Hope* and *As My Parents Age*


"Not often can you read a book so honest and feel so at home. Readers will
sense the courage it took for Billie Jauss to push past a surface life to one of
depth and want to go right there with her. Through her authentic sharing,
she offers insight and an invitation for us to recognize how we too can make
room for a life led beautifully, intentionally, and uniquely set part for God. An
inspiring read!"

—Jan Kern, author, speaker, life coach,
and founder of Voice of Courage (voiceofcourage.org)


"This book is a must-read for those of us who confuse doing with being. So
many nuggets of truth are tucked away in these pages."

—Gari Meacham, author of *Truly Fed, Spirit Hunger,*
and *Be Free*, president of The Vine Uganda


"Billie lives life with such full-throttle passion yet she has learned how to listen
to the 'holy nudge' that directs one to God's blueprints. As a recovering control
freak, I smiled as I read the process of Billie learning the liberating truth of
doing less so God can do more. Billie inspires the reader to release the firm grip
on one's blueprints and with open palms accept the 'Papa Approved' script for
one's life! I applaud your transparency, Billie!"

—Jackie Kendall, president of Power to Grow Inc.,
author of *Surrender Your Jr. God Badge*

"*Making Room* is a compass for anyone who wants to learn to fall in love with Jesus and find true joy in your life. Billie not only writes from the heart, she lives it! You need to make time for *Making Room*."

—Rod Olson, author of *The Legacy Builder* and *The Wisdom Lunch Warrior*

"I first met Billie Jauss when she graciously hosted me in her home for a World Vision Women of Vision event in Florida. While her life was busy, I immediately recognized a woman eager to allow God to use her to make a difference. Willingness to be inconvenienced, stretched, and moved out of our comfort zones is always the key to seeing God make us change agents in this desperate world, and for this reason I found Billie Jauss's honest account of her own personal journey a relatable and inspiring read. I encourage anyone who feels they are too busy, inadequate, or irrelevant to change the world in Jesus' name to read *Making Room*!"

—Marilee Pierce Dunker, international speaker and author of *Man of Vision*

# Making Room

## Doing Less So God Can Do More

### Billie Jauss

*Many Blessings!*
*Billie Jauss*
*Eph. 3:20*

**NEW HOPE**
PUBLISHERS
Gospel-Centered. Missions-Driven.

BIRMINGHAM, ALABAMA

New Hope® Publishers
PO Box 12065
Birmingham, AL 35202-2065
NewHopePublishers.com
New Hope Publishers is a division of WMU®.

Making Room: Doing Less So God Can Do More
© 2018 by Billie Jauss
All rights reserved. First printing 2018.
Printed in the United States of America.

New Hope Publishers serves its authors as they express their views, which may not express the views of the publisher.

Library of Congress Cataloging-in-Publication Data

Names: Jauss, Billie, 1966- author.
Title: Making room : doing less so God can do more / Billie Jauss.
Description: First [edition]. | Birmingham : New Hope Publishers, 2017.
Identifiers: LCCN 2017030966 | ISBN 9781625915351 (permabind)
Subjects: LCSH: Christian life. | Spirituality--Christianity. | Spiritual
  life--Christianity. | Holy Spirit.
Classification: LCC BV4501.3 .J38 2017 | DDC 248.4--dc23
LC record available at https://lccn.loc.gov/2017030966

(Copyright information continues on p. 188.)

ISBN-13: 978-1-62591-535-1

N184108 • 1017 • 2.5M1

# gratitude

**I owe tremendous gratitude to the two women who launched me into this writing journey.**

Bev Sparling, we met while sitting by a pool in Arizona during the Pro Athlete's Outreach Conference. You encouraged me to write about my life experiences in baseball for Baseball Chapel Devotions. With your editorial prowess, you made me look like a writer. Your guidance created a desire to pen more devotions—the beginning of my writing "career." Thank you.

Katharine Grubb, the 10 Minute Novelist, we have seen a lot of life together. We have cried (mostly you), talked, and prayed for each other through the years. The word spoken over both of us, about writing, was what you knew for your entire life and I had no idea for mine. Fast-forward many years. You needed a guinea pig for your book, *Write a Novel in 10 Minutes a Day*. The experience was eye-opening and career-changing. You showed me a love for writing in a deeper way. Thank you.

# Contents

# Acknowledgments

Thanks abound from a grateful heart . . .

First and foremost I thank God for giving a little girl from an Eastern North Carolina farm the gumption to never give up, the love of learning, and a desire to live life to the fullest with Him.

Thank you to my husband of many years for loving me no matter what, being my biggest encourager, and believing in me when I couldn't. Life is more joyous with you. I never knew how exciting life could be, and then there was baseball. There is never a dull moment in the traveling Jauss house. God's love shines through you more every day. I look forward to the rest of our lives glorifying Him and loving each other through this crazy baseball life.

Thank you to my three wonderful babies who aren't babies anymore. To the one who made me a mom, DJ, you challenge me every day. Your love is felt deeply even from the great distances you travel and live. My middle baby, Charley, your heart is bigger and more caring than I could have prayed for when you were born. Thank you for your constant encouragement. My baby boy, Will, you are special and strong-willed, a mini-me of your father and my miracle. God gave you to us when we didn't think there would be another. I thank Him daily. The three of you have been such an encouragement throughout this process. When I didn't think I could do it, you gave me courage. I am so proud of the men you have become.

Thank you to my mama. Watching you read late into the nights spawned a love of reading and books. I hope you enjoy this one.

Thank you to my sister JoAnne. Your love is immeasurable. I thank God you had a large hand in raising me. I think I turned out pretty good.

Thank you to my Dream Team of Prayer Warriors: Debi, Fran, Ingrid,

Jan, Jeannine, Marcia, and Rene. The prayers were felt at the most needed of times. Knowing you all were going to God for this book and His words to be written was an incredible encouragement and support.

Thank you to New Hope Publishers and Mark Bethea for offering that little girl turned nearly 50-year-old a book contract. A dream I never knew I had came true.

Thank you to my editor, Ramona Richards.

Thank you to my agent, Wendy Lawton at Books & Such Literary Management. You are strength in this complex pathway to publishing. Thank you for walking with me.

Thank you to Gari Meacham, fellow baseball wife and teacher of the next steps toward publishing. Your advice and experience are invaluable.

Thank you to Jan Kern for not throwing me out of your preconference nonfiction class when I freaked out over the overall story of my book. Your kind spirit and gentle support have been a steadying foundation for me throughout this process.

Thank you to Gail Mills, my personal editor, friend, and mentor. You have been a dear friend for many years. Your talent for editing crafted a better book than I thought I could create. I am forever grateful for your encouragement and supportive relationship.

Thank you to Debi Tunney, my prayer partner during highs and lows. We don't always get to connect each week, but I know you are there, when I am weak, to point me to Jesus.

# PART 1 | Preparing to Be Moved by the Holy Spirit

# Evaluation of the Heart

## CHAPTER ONE

"What is God doing in and through you?" our pastor asked. My head flew up; the chair groaned as I shifted in my seat. Blood thundered in my ears as my heart pounded. I thought, *What? Well, let me make a list of all the great things He is doing in and through me.* Defensive, yes. Convicted, not yet. Shaken up, definitely. Complacency had taken over my desire to grow deeper with God. Life was comfortable, but what was I allowing Him to do in and through me?

I began making a long and fulfilling mental list. *Things aren't too hard. I have a stable marriage. My boys aren't in any current trouble. Everyone is healthy.* God was doing a lot. I was the one not allowing Him near.

The reality was my busy life stood in the way of my connection with Jesus. With a sports-filled schedule, a Bible study wasn't on my calendar. I picked up my Bible and took it to church, placing it on a table when I returned home. It stayed there until the next Sunday, unless I was going to a Bible study, and that wasn't happening. I prayed when I felt I *needed* to. I didn't see anything wrong with my life choices. I wasn't making immoral decisions. My life was busy.

I left church, like I do many Sundays, with my checklist of things I needed to do. Church was checked off—and I was on to the next thing. Throughout the day the question my pastor posed kept nagging at me like a stray hair. You can't quite get hold of it, and when you do, it flies right back up your nose.

"What was God doing in and through me?" Knowing this was going to be a spiritual journey, I tried to push the question deeper and further into my head and spirit, but God would not allow me to push it too far. He knew—and eventually I knew—the preparation of this spiritual adventure would have to begin in my heart.

Once I was home and the house was quiet, I opened my Bible to the verse our pastor had referenced. "Now to him who is able to do immeasurably more than all we ask or imagine, according to his power that is at work within us" (Ephesians 3:20). The meatiness of this one verse lay heavy on my heart. The quietness of the house that night made me wonder if my sleeping family could hear my heart beat. I absorbed the words, the promise of Christ. I opened my journal and began to write.

"Now to him who is able." I read the words, emphasizing *Him. He* is able. *He* wants us to focus on *Him* and *His* ability. So I asked myself whether or not I viewed God as the Almighty Powerful or if I believed my abilities, lists, and accomplishments were enough. Did my actions blind me to what He wanted to do in my life? Did my choices reveal a heart that aligned itself every day with His Word and His ability?

Many of the choices I make are good choices, but then there are the not-so-good choices—the ones that make me feel guilty or inadequate. I know I often lack a healthy balance in my life. I ride the wave of success, enjoying the joys that come with it in one moment, then fall to the feeling of failure when things don't work out the way I think they should.

Do we impede the power of God by puffing up on the joys of success or crushing under the weight of failure? Do our circumstances hinder His ability to work in and through us? Do we hamper His mighty power by trying to do everything on our own?

When I find myself in a negative situation, I tend to shut down. Whether it's my child not choosing the right path, my husband being let go from a team, seeing a negative comment on my blog, receiving a rejection of a book idea, or experiencing anything that interferes with my plan or ideal, negative thoughts, worries, and fears replay over and over again in my head. Rather than changing the direction of my thoughts through prayer, I become paralyzed and refuse to give my circumstance to God.

But even when things were going great, I didn't tend to pray. I saw positive circumstances as blessings from God and negatives as responses to my failure. My ability to view God as the Almighty only revealed itself when it was convenient to my emotions and circumstances. I needed to realign my perspective of His mighty power. I noted in my journal, "Not to us, Lord, not to us but to your name be the glory, because of your love and faithfulness" (Psalm 115:1).

I returned to the next part of the Ephesians passage, "to do immeasurably more than all we ask or imagine." When I embraced God's ability and almighty power, this promise of Scripture began to reveal God's desires in and through my life. God is always at work. He is a God of action. He can do more than we are capable of even fathoming in our human brain. He is not inhibited or limited by our ineptness or failure. He remains all-powerful.

God wants to work in and through us to glorify Him and to benefit His kingdom. The plan may not be the way we envision but it is the most beneficial for God's plan. "And God is able to bless you abundantly, so that in all things at all times, having all that you need, you will abound in every good work" (2 Corinthians 9:8). God wants to do immeasurably more in His ability to equip us for His good works.

Dreams are the fuel for driving us toward a goal. We dream about our future, our plan for life, our next adventure, and things we want. What if the biggest dream we could even imagine was too small for

God? God fulfilled dreams I had in the past more abundantly than I could have imagined. The man I married, the children God entrusted to me, the godly friends I'm surrounded by, and each wonderful, spiritual experience were only a few of the blessings God provided. God's provisions are grander than anything I could have dreamed.

I had evidence of God's bountiful provision, so why did I find it hard to believe He was capable of working in my life again? God is always working in, through, and around us. Our responsibility requires us to get out of the way and allow Him to be God. I believed it in my head, but my heart was not following. I could recite promises from God from my memory, yet my heart didn't absorb them in my actions. I kept holding on to my ability, not His.

The final portion of the Ephesians passage reads, "according to his power that is at work within us." His power *already works* within us. God desires to tap us into His power and accomplish what only He can do. He desires obedience and wants us to turn all our control over to Him. To say "yes!" to Him.

As I reflected on God's desire to work in me, my mind was flooded by memories of when I thought I was in control. I was overwhelmed. How many times had I run ahead with my own desires, leaving God in my dust? I underestimated His ability and power at work in me. By underestimating His power at work in me, I stood in the way of the work only He could accomplish.

My spirit ached for God's presence. The knowledge of God's ability, power, and desire brought me to a realization. Our inner life—our heart's alignment with the will of God—is of utmost importance. So preparation for this spiritual adventure needed to start with an evaluation of the heart.

Every minute five liters of blood takes a journey through our heart, veins, and arteries to provide the oxygen our bodies need to keep us alive and healthy—a vital function necessary to sustaining life. And all of this happens without us even having to think about it. While erratic or dysfunctional heartbeats can happen without symptoms, a person can live with asymptomatic rhythms.

Similarly, our spiritual heart can malfunction without immediate symptoms. We can become comfortable with our faith, even complacent at times. As we grow in our Bible knowledge and become familiar with prayer, we may not pick up our Bibles as often and sometimes pray on the fly.

Volunteering and giving may be our passion, but there are times when writing a check is easier than committing time. And we may think our circumstances reflect our spiritual life. So when life is good, it must be because we are taking the right spiritual dosage. We are on top of all things chaotic and flitting.

God was waking me up and redefining my understanding of Him. He kept reminding me that He is never finished. "What is God doing in and through you?" My heart beat with force and fervor.

I love lists. So in order to decipher my pastor's question and what God was trying to teach me, I quickly took to my journal. I thought it would make me feel better once the lists were on paper. I began with two columns. I labeled one *IN* for what God was doing in me and the other *THROUGH* for what God was doing through me. A bright yellow highlighter was used to emphasize the two titles.

**IN**
- I read my Bible.
- I pray and try to listen.
- I try to be obedient in my actions and my speech.

**THROUGH**
- I lead Bible studies.
- I write a Christian blog.
- I write devotions for women through Baseball Chapel.
- I serve.

Looking more closely at the IN list didn't help my heart. I try to read my Bible consistently, but I get busy. I pray but mostly when I am afraid or need something to turn out the way I want. I'm obedient . . . mostly. That is until I'm driving in traffic. Then my actions and words aren't always godly.

I had similar reactions to the THROUGH list. The list was what I was in control of, what I was accomplishing in my strength. Where was God? What was I allowing Him to do? Was I missing the most important thing I could be doing? Could I allow God full access and control of every aspect of my life?

*I am not a selfish person. I serve God. I do good things,* I thought.

Again, I responded defensively. The lists revealed a truth that was not pleasing; my life had become shallow and self-centered. All of the accomplishments were self-focused, not God-focused.

My abilities and my need for control had overtaken my life. Life had become busy raising three boys, keeping up with the demands of my husband's baseball schedule, the kids' activities, volunteering, leading Bible studies, writing, and the many other responsibilities where I felt I was in control. The choices did not involve guidance from God. They were all activities on a checklist to fill my sons' schedules and desires, my husband's career, or things that made me feel as though my life was purposeful and fulfilled. Life was going well this way. Or was it?

I questioned God with every heartbeat. Why did He have to come in and rock my comfortable Christian life? The realization of having fallen into a life that took me to places I never intended to go stopped me in my tracks. My spiritual life was about to be shaken up. God would not let me be satisfied stuck in defense of my actions. Life had become personally driven, not God-guided.

I knew I wasn't where I should be in my faith. I was relying on human wisdom and not God's power. I only knew one way to begin to redirect my focus. Have you ever asked God to guide you through Scripture and then read a passage—maybe one you've read many times—and felt a new and fresh understanding? I opened my Bible again to Ephesians 3. Where the question that sparked this journey lay.

Imprisoned because of his faith, the Apostle Paul wrote to the Ephesians about what it meant, in faith and practice, to be a Christian—regardless of circumstances. Paul had spent most of his life teaching the Gentile Christians. He taught them they were to stand like a rock for their freedom in Christ. Paul did not see two churches, the Jewish and the Gentile, but one church unified in Christ.

Paul said Christ was inclusive, welcoming everyone. He admonished, though, that as we approach Him freely, we must be willing to learn and grow according to His Word. Christ was the one who had the power to solve all problems and bring unity to all. Paul was against the religion of human attainment. He taught the divine provision of salvation by faith in God. God provides what we could never attain.

Paul wanted the recipients of his letters to know Christ better. He told them of the Christ who enables believers to have the power that resurrected Jesus. When we are saved by grace, this power comes to us through His Spirit. Being one with Christ allows His power within us.

When we believe our ability is more reliable than God, we discount His power to work within us. It broke my heart to know I was obstructing God's power and guidance. When did I allow life to take me to a place of not growing deeper with God? When did I stop listening to His guidance? When did my heart become stagnant? I left Him out of my busy life, only connecting with him to get what I wanted. I prayed the prayers of my heart's desires, not His desires for me. A huge wall had been built between God and me, inhibiting His power at work in and through me.

In our busyness, we often divide our lives into what involves God and what doesn't. We keep what we can in control and don't ask for

Jesus' guidance in the minutiae of life. When we do find a need to invite Him in, we often don't take the time to wait patiently. We ask for His guidance but get too busy to listen. We think to ask for help but push it aside thinking others are more in need than us. I saw I had created this division in my heart.

With heartfelt prayer I began asking—begging—God to show me the root of the problem. He reminded me. The small whisper of God spoke deeply into my spirit, "It's a heart matter."

Our hearts are the hubs of our souls. Consider the role of our physical hearts—they signal our brains and alter our emotional responses. These signals increase attention, perception, problem solving, and memory. Alternately, erratic and disordered physical heart rate patterns limit our ability to think clearly, remember events, learn, and make life decisions. Stress can lead to impulsive and unwise decisions. Our minds are clearer when under less stress. Similarly, our spiritual hearts play a vital role in our thinking, ambition, emotions, and moral decisions. Unguarded hearts affect our entire being. Heart signals become distorted, invading our spiritual lives with clutter.

My heart was the problem. The division of what was in my control and where I thought God was allowed was sending unhealthy signals from my heart to my soul. I had allowed outside influences— complacency, comfort, distractions, and busyness—to distort healthy spiritual heart signals. The time spent evaluating my heart, figuring out what lay in the crevices, the spaces the Holy Spirit should be occupying, would take me out of my comfort zone. Healthy growth happens when we are outside our comfort zone, and I was speeding quickly into uncomfortable territory. Not really where I wanted to go but desperately needed in order to venture in that direction.

In Ephesians 3, Paul wrote about the mystery of Christ revealed to him and how we share in the promises of Christ. Because of Christ, we can draw nearer to God than ever before: "In him and through faith in him we may approach God with freedom and confidence" (v. 12). The open road was laid before me, and God beckoned me to be available and trust, accept His freedom, and have the confidence to approach Him.

When we become comfortable and complacent in our Christian walk, our belief in Jesus as our Savior becomes a bit murky. Our busy lives overwhelm us and take over the direction of our decisions and choices. The division between God and our hearts becomes vast. We leave our hearts unguarded. Trash moves in and our beliefs become altered.

I had become comfortable and complacent. Earnestly praying for guidance, I knew He would carry me to—and carry me through—an honest evaluation of my heart. Exposing the depths of my heart would reveal what I wholeheartedly believed, the foundation of my Christian life—Christ is my Savior.

As Christians, we know Christ died on the Cross for the forgiveness of our sins. He was buried and rose from the dead, offering salvation for all who believe in Him. Through faith, we have a unique opportunity to walk in relationship with Him. Having a relationship with Jesus is more than adhering to a bunch of do's and don'ts. This relationship is not about being perfect but about becoming closer to Him and learning His ways. As our relationship grows with Christ, the choices in our life will be more Christlike because God is more powerful than anything we can ever imagine.

Seeking a personal relationship with Christ is the best decision I have ever made, and I pray that for you as well. When we commit our lives to Jesus and accept Him as our Savior, the power of renewal is promised. Our old grimy lives are gone. We are a new creation. "Therefore, if anyone is in Christ, the new creation has come: The old has gone, the new is here!" (2 Corinthians 5:17).

This passage is one we have heard and read, but it's not always easy to see the old as gone. Our past and current mistakes are products of a sinful nature: "For all have sinned and fall short of the glory of God" (Romans 3:23). We will sin. The question is how we will react to sin. *Lord, enlighten the dark in me.* Two directions become clear: shame or conviction. They are easily confused and drastically different.

*Shame* is a painful emotion caused by consciousness of guilt, shortcoming, or impropriety; a condition of humiliating disgrace or disrepute; something to be regretted. Shame is an emotion based on our feelings, our regret of doing something that makes us feel worthless, of feeling unworthy of the love of God, an embarrassing action of not glorifying God. The reaction of shame is directed at us.

I have carried shame with me. Asking God for forgiveness, I would feel peace, only to be reminded of the same mistakes and return to the shame of my past. I read books on spiritual healing that suggested making a list of things from my shameful past and burning it as a symbolic gesture of moving forward. I did so, only to have the shame continue to haunt me. Memories stumped my growth in maturity toward Christ and in the knowledge of how He could use me.

What begins as an emotional response of feeling unworthy often leads to avoidance of God Himself. This response is the enemy's attempt at keeping us as far away from God as possible. Shame leads us to live on our ability, not God's power.

"Yet the LORD longs to be gracious to you; therefore he will rise up to show you compassion. For the LORD is a God of justice. Blessed are all who wait for him!" (Isaiah 30:18). God is a compassionate and relational God. He longs to be gracious to us. Choosing to seek God and build a relationship with Him allows us to begin to discern between shame and conviction.

*Conviction* is a firmly held belief or opinion. It comes in the small whispers of God telling us the things we have done wrong are a starting point in growing closer to Him. With it comes the urge to ask for forgiveness and focus on His healing power in our lives. It allows us to seek the answer God has for us in our search to glorify Him. Conviction is all about the power of Christ. Shame is all about self. Shame shows us the problem. Conviction shows us the answer.

As we begin to see the difference between shame and conviction, we can take the focus off ourselves and redirect it on Christ. Keeping our eyes on Jesus drives our desire to honestly answer the question, "What is God doing in and through me?" *Lord, lead us into a deeper relationship with You, revealing Your will for my life, allowing Your spirit to roam freely within me and outwardly to others.*

Another heart matter is the world of knowledge and lure of prosperity. We are bombarded with go, go, go, gain, gain, gain. How many times do we hear from others that pay increases, a new car, and a new job are blessings from God—or a sickness, an accident, and being demoted are attacks of the enemy? Society's focus is on prosperity; we look to God for material and financial gain.

Living as the wife of a Major League Baseball (MLB) coach, there are many times the lures of possessions, labels, cars, homes, clothes, and prosperity are very powerful. When another wife comes into the ballpark with a new Louis Vuitton purse or Prada shoes or I see a player's son with his iPad or stroll past a player's new Tesla in the parking lot, the temptation is to compare and acquire. Our family cannot afford these things, nor do we need them, but the desire for the next best thing can crash my spirit like an avalanche. I would even pray God would give my husband a raise or rationalize that a little more debt wouldn't hurt.

We don't have to be in the MLB to find ourselves wanting what others have. The neighbor puts in a new sprinkler system and their grass starts looking like a country club golf course. They buy a new car, new fishing boat, leather sectional, or great vacation, and we can feel an instant and intense sense of desire and need. Whatever the item we desire, the neighbor, friend, or family member will obtain it. We have a need to fill our materialistic urgings. Those desires flood our minds while we get further and further away from God's desires for us. They invade the deep spaces of our souls where the Holy Spirit should freely roam. The desires become all-consuming, robbing us of the power of the Holy Spirit and joy.

How can we get past those desires? God demonstrated His love for us by sending His Son to die on a Cross. His love for us is amazing. His power in us is immeasurable. His power guides us away from our desires to His.

The first question in the Bible asked by God was, "Where are you?" (Genesis 3:9). God asked it after Eve took the fruit from the tree, ate it, and shared it with Adam. Their sin revealed their nakedness. They felt shame. Sewing fig leaves to cover themselves, they heard God and hid. God knew where they were. He asked, "Where are you?" He did not question their location. God knew where they were. God directed the question to the position of their heart. Where were their hearts? With this first sin, immediate separation from God occurred. Their hearts separated them from God.

God asks us the same question. Where are you? Are we making ourselves available to Him? Have we restricted our lives, not allowing our spirit to be open to Him? Have busyness and distractions pulled us away from Jesus?

As we dig deeper, evaluating our heart, it can become overwhelming. Exposing the true depths of our hearts brings us closer to a deeper connection with Christ, but revealing what lies in the depths can be painful. "Here I am! I stand at the door and knock. If anyone hears my voice and opens the door, I will come in and eat with that person, and they with me" (Revelation 3:20).

God is interested more in our relationship with Him than any checklist of past wrongs or hurts. He has forgiven us of those. His concern includes the condition of our heart, our connection with Him. Have you found a time in your life when you question, *who am I?*

When I was a child, a popular question where I grew up was, "Who's your daddy?" I knew Bill was my daddy and Bet was my mama. I knew I was the little sister of Cathy, Eddie, Benny, JoAnne, David, Denise, and Helen. When I went away to college, I was a nursing student and a Delta Zeta sorority sister. Then after marriage, I was Dave Jauss's wife. When I had children, I was always DJ, Charley, and Will's mom.

In the time since my youngest son went off to college, I have found a great deal of the identity I held on to for many years was displaced. I was no longer involved in the many activities I had been with my kids. I was pursuing my goals, mine and mine alone. At a writer's conference, I was asked by a publisher, "Who are you?" It was the first time I didn't have a ready-made answer of an ownership connected to my family.

For me, identifying myself by my place in a family, by birth or by marriage was a quick answer of belonging. These answers weren't about who I was a person—my identity—but an identifier of where I belonged. Once those seasons were in my past, however, I had to think, *who am I really?* Being confident in who I am has never been a struggle for me, but when the publisher asked me, my answer was not so quick and self-assured.

Who am I in the empty nest? I am my husband's wife. With his prominent job as a Major League Baseball coach, I cannot avoid the label of being Dave Jauss's wife! I continue to be my children's mother. I will always be my daddy and mama's daughter and the baby of my family. However, now in another season, I needed to identify who I am.

Who am I? I am a child of God. I know this to the core of my being. I am strong and confident because of my faith. I am a proud wife of an amazing husband I love dearly and like most of the time! He is the man God gave me to dance with through this life.

I am a writer. To admit this to myself was much harder than the writing process. I began to embrace the gift God has given me and use it to glorify him. I am a mother—a mother who no longer needs to oversee every aspect of my children's lives. I am a mentor and guide for my kids through the young adult years of their lives.

Identifying who we are begins with trusting God with who He has created us to be. Understanding that above all the chaos and confusion, He has a plan and hope for our future. He has gone before us to prepare the way. When the seasons of our lives change and we question who we are, we turn to Him for our identity. Standing strong and confident in who He has created us to be, to glorify Him, guides us to use the gifts we have been given to continue to move forward

We are His.

We are strong.

We are living life to the fullest.

As seasons change and life continues, we grab onto our faith and let God pull us along. Life can take us into places where our identity is displaced. God has been there before us. Knowing who we are in Him helps in the changing seasons defining our lives. We can trust that God has a plan and hope for our future.

> *All this is from God, who reconciled us to himself through Christ and gave us the ministry of reconciliation: that God was reconciling the world to himself in Christ, not counting people's sins against them. And he has committed to us the message of reconciliation. We are therefore Christ's ambassadors, as though God were making his appeal through us. We implore you on Christ's behalf: Be reconciled to God.*
>
> *—2 Corinthians 5:18–20*

The old self, our spiritual self before we believed, was a slave to sin and death. Our new self is forgiven and free, given the gift of grace. Our sinful spirits have been destroyed; our slates have been wiped clean. Sin no longer controls us, His Spirit does. Even though our past has been wiped clean, we have to choose every day to live in the freedom of knowing Christ was sacrificed for us.

Reconciliation is a restoration of friendly relations. Isn't it what we want with Jesus, a friendly relationship? If we are to have this type of relationship with Almighty God, He has to cleanse our hearts of the past so we can choose to live in His love and forgiveness. Getting rid of our old selves and walking in the new selves is a gift of our faith.

"You are my portion, LORD; I have promised to obey your words" (Psalm 119:57). He is our portion. Jesus satisfies our needs better than a bigger house, a name-brand dress, or any amount of money. When the Lord becomes our portion, He moves in powerful ways. Remembering God is our portion isn't always easy. God meets us where we are. He cleanses our hearts to be more open to His desires.

The evaluation of the heart reveals the malfunctions can be asymptomatic until we find ourselves where we never intended to be—in critical condition, complacent, and lacking the desire to grow deeper with Christ and experience abundance in Him. The evaluation of our hearts increases our desires for a permanent pursuit of God, not of personal pleasure.

The spiritual journey that began with the question, "What is God doing in and through you," didn't begin because it was easy. I had no desire to go off the course of my comfortable Christian life. The journey began because I truly wanted to know the immeasurably more God desires to do in and through me. Looking at the condition of my heart was the beginning of my spiritual travel, an adventure long overdue.

# *Distractions*

## CHAPTER TWO

The first time I sent my youngest off to school wasn't to kindergarten when he was five. It was when he was 13 and headed to seventh grade. After we had homeschooled for seven years, we packed up and moved to a sunnier climate and enrolled him in a traditional public school. New to the area and seeing all the extra time I would have on my hands, I packed my schedule with volunteering, babysitting, lunches, chairing organizations, and a part-time job.

Six months later I could barely get myself out of bed. Exhausted and lonely, I realized I had taken on too much—and too many of the wrong things. It was when I was sinking into the despair of circumstances and overwhelmed with busyness that I felt far from God. Where was He? Why did He seem so far away? I was going to church and attending a Bible study. What was happening?

It had been a few years since our middle son left for college when this spiritual journey began. The impending empty nest was looming large. My husband and I had talked about what the empty nest looked like for our marriage, but I had not begun to evaluate what it looked like for me individually. I had been a full-time, stay-at-home mom for more than 15 years after many fulfilling years as an intensive care nurse. When I looked at the next season of life, I could only envision a big black hole with no direction or purpose. What did the future look like without kids in the house? How would I handle it? There would be so much unoccupied time.

I knew I didn't want to feel separated from God again. I knew vacant time would infiltrate the empty nest, just as it had when my youngest went to school. Any sort of transition can do that. But vacant time should be an opportunity to be filled with the righteous pursuit of God, not my personal pursuit of schedule fillers. I needed to identify the distractions I allowed to fill my schedule and my spirit.

This journey came in God's perfect timing. He knew the impending empty nest was rocking my world. I knew I had to identify the distractions in my life. I was embracing the identity of spiritual traveler, seeking the answers that could only come from him.

Baseball travel, following my husband from one Major League city to another, filled my life schedule. The spiritual adventure I was embarking on was not on my schedule, but I knew I had to add it. The necessity of the expedition into the distant parts of my soul was essential. I didn't like where I was in my faith. I knew I needed to rectify my spiritual complacency. Let the adventure begin.

"The Big Rocks of Life" by Stephen Covey is a story of an expert speaking to a group of business students. The expert brought out a one-gallon, wide-mouthed Mason jar. He began to fill the jar with fist-sized rocks, carefully adding one at a time. When he had finished, he asked the overachieving class if the jar was full. They acknowledged it was.

Next, the expert pulled out a jar of gravel and proceeded to pour the gravel into the jar. He gently shook the jar, and the gravel filled the spaces between the big rocks. He asked again if the jar was full. By this point the class was pessimistic—knowing the expert was teaching a greater lesson. Then, he poured sand that filled the spaces between the gravel and big rocks; the class knew the jar wasn't full.

Finally, he produced a pitcher of water and poured it into the jar, filling it to the top.

The point of this illustration isn't that no matter how full our schedule is we can always add more. Rather, if we don't put the big rocks in first, they will never fit. The distractions that filled our jar (our spirit) were taking up space our big rock, Jesus, needed to be. We need to place Jesus at the center of our soul first.

The jar of my spiritual life was going to have larger spaces to fill once my son went to college. Knowing the big rock, Jesus, needed to go first was a vital first step, but I also needed to identify the other space fillers—the distractions—that were taking up the empty space. No matter the type of diversion, they can lead to a place of wasted opportunities for the Lord.

Filling my time with many different opportunities to stay busy left me too occupied to see the work God wanted to do in me. We can miss these experiences God gives us to refine our spirit. A small whisper to talk to the woman sitting next to you, to ask about her story, asking to hold a baby, or maybe even turning down someone's offer to help because you think you would have to return the favor. Are we making ourselves available for the Lord? Are we filling our spirit with a list of to-dos, not allowing Him to fill our soul?

How many opportunities does God present when we don't take the time to see or hear because we have filled our jar with busyness? This busyness takes up the room those larger rocks are meant to fill. We fill our souls with meetings, lunches, volunteering, and working. All of these things are useful and necessary to connect and be successful in life, but when we push God out of the center of our soul, we end up overwhelmed and undernourished.

It's time to evaluate these wasted experiences and see just how much we are ignoring the Lord's guidance. It's time to place those big rocks in first and replenish our spirits. What a mighty God we serve!

I continue to pray the distractions of this life do not overpower His mighty power throughout my life and your life.

The clutter of life fills the stagnant areas within us. It begins simply. These distractions pull us away from building a deeper relationship with Christ and seeing clearly the opportunities He has put in front of us. The distractions take up residence within us, drawing us deeper and deeper, further and further from our connection with Him.

Distractions are inevitable, and some distractions need to be prioritized in different seasons of our life. However, we must be aware of the separation distractions can cause from our connection with the Lord. We need to stay focused. "I have hidden your word in my heart that I might not sin against you" (Psalm 119:11).

When I looked at what I was filling my jar with, I determined I was filling it with many things that God hadn't given me to fill it with. And when I looked at the distractions, at those issues, I felt guilty. I had failed. Once again I was controlling my life and not allowing God to direct my steps. While my first instinct in moments of failure is to shut down, this time, with my purposeful intent to continue my journey, I pushed the negative thoughts away and continued to search my heart and life. I needed to honestly identify where I was too busy and where I was wasting opportunity.

Again I turned to lists. Yes, I know I have a problem with pen and paper and lists upon lists. But the list was going to help me identify the internal and external distractions. I used it to list my own experiences as well as the experiences of women I talked with about the distractions in their lives. We shared similarities. This list was in no way exhaustive. However, it helped identify the internal and external distractions that take up space in our spirits. I started with . . .

## "I DESERVE"

When we stopped homeschooling, I felt I deserved time off. I had earned lunch with friends. I deserved to watch television or nap. Those rewards of what I "deserved" started with good intentions and a commitment to getting back to reading my Bible and doing a daily devotion . . . in a week or so. It was months before I realized I still only moved my Bible when I took it to church on Sundays. Occasionally, I picked it up for a weekly Bible study I didn't consistently attend. It was never opened for one-on-one time with the Lord during the week. I had uncovered this same behavior when I was evaluating my heart at the beginning of this journey . . . repeat behavior I needed to rectify.

What I thought I *deserved* filled up the time of what I *needed*, which was time with Jesus to align my heart to His and fill my soul with love and peace. I had kept such a tight schedule while we were homeschooling I thought that now I deserved rewards for all my hard work. But what I chose to reward myself with only led to spiritual malnourishment. What we believe we deserve becomes the big rock in our jar. What we often overlook, however, is that what we really deserve is to be punished for our wrongdoings in life. But God gave forgiveness when Jesus died on the Cross. We are saved from eternal death! That's one of our big rocks—the fact that we didn't get what we deserve.

## WORRY

Oh, the burden of worry. I grew up in a house of worry. If there was nothing to worry about, my mother would create something. It didn't matter the subject—her kids, money, the house, others—it didn't matter. She worried. She lived in a "what-if" world. My mom thought you were not normal if you weren't worrying about something. Living in these circumstances made worry a constant presence in my life. I didn't want worry to control me, but it did. And like my mother, so much of what we worry about is created. We waste so much time distracted by worry about possible circumstances that never happen.

God does not want us to worry. "Do not be afraid" is one of the most-used phrases in the Bible. God takes care of us, yet the concerns for our future and our needs often overwhelm our thoughts:

> If that is how God clothes the grass of the field, which is here today and tomorrow is thrown into the fire, will he not much more clothe you—you of little faith? So do not worry, saying, "What shall we eat?" or "What shall we drink?" or "What shall we wear?" For the pagans run after all these things, and your heavenly Father knows that you need them. But seek first his kingdom and his righteousness, and all these things will be given to you as well. Therefore do not worry about tomorrow, for tomorrow will worry about itself. Each day has enough trouble of its own.
>
> —Matthew 6:30–35

Still, I worry. Worry tells us we need to take control out of God's hands and try to hold all the power in ours (at least we think we can). But seek first His kingdom. Seek Him first, and all these things will be given to us as well. What a promise!

## NEGATIVE THOUGHTS

Negative thoughts like worry can turn our minds into a flurry of emotional torment. We bombard ourselves with thoughts of *what if?* Negative, anxious, or doubtful thoughts are common in the Christian community as much as they are in secular society. Just because we believe in Christ doesn't mean you are immune to struggles. But Christian have the advantage of knowing where we can turn for help and comfort. When we identify the negative, we can turn to Scripture—and Jesus—for help in replacing them with a more positive mind-set. This is not Pollyanna-type "positive thinking." It's recognizing the good things in our lives and knowing that God leads us through all trials, right beside us. "Finally, brothers and sisters, whatever is true, whatever is noble, whatever is right, whatever is pure, whatever is lovely, whatever is admirable— if anything is excellent or praiseworthy—think about such things" (Philippians 4:8).

## LACK OF FORGIVENESS

The inability to forgive another is a fatal poison that separates us from a holy God. It divides us from prayer, worship, healing, and forgiveness. In a story from the Book of Matthew, a king is seeking repayment of debt from his servant. The servant asks the king to be patient with him and the king shows patience by canceling his debt. But then the servant turns and demands a much smaller repayment of debt from a fellow servant:

> *Then the master called the servant. "You wicked servant," he said, "I canceled all that debt of yours because you begged me to. Shouldn't you*

*have had mercy on your fellow servant just as I had on you?" In anger his master handed him over to the jailers to be tortured, until he should pay back all he owed. "This is how my heavenly Father will treat each of you unless you forgive your brother or sister from your heart."*

—Matthew 18:32–35

The servant was turned over to torture because he was not showing the same forgiveness the king gave.

When we do not forgive, we are turned over to torture also—the torture of depression, fear, anxiety, and loneliness. We forgive for our benefit, not to show mercy. While we may have to set boundaries with those who have harmed us, we must forgive because God first forgave us. And we not only need to forgive others, we need to forgive ourselves.

For a long time, I held on to things in my past. I had not fully released them to God. Yes, I "laid them at the foot of the Cross" and "handed them to the Lord," but for some crazy reason, I continued to pick them back up and carry them around. Our past has certainly influenced us, but it doesn't have to define us. "If we confess our sins, he is faithful and just and will forgive us our sins and purify us from all unrighteousness" (1 John 1:9).

## ANGER

The internal distraction of anger can start out slowly only to escalate into a consuming rage. It's inevitable. Certain events in our lives cause us to become angry. These experiences happen. We get upset. Feel hurt, wronged, unfairly treated. We experience pain. Having these feelings is not the problem.

They are natural. The problem arises when these feelings build up and inflict verbal and physical pain on others. Being consumed by anger makes us question God, and we choose to push Him away.

We defend our actions. As we sit and stew over our feelings, allowing the anger to build, we continue to separate ourselves from God. "Refrain from anger and turn from wrath; do not fret—it leads only to evil" (Psalm 37:8). It isn't possible to dwell in anger and not sin in our thoughts or actions. "My dear brothers and sisters, take note of this: Everyone should be quick to listen, slow to speak and slow to become angry" (James 1:19).

## COMPARISON

As I continued to dig around my soul for other distractions, a friend showed up to my house in her shiny new car carrying a purse that was made of the most beautiful brown, supple leather. And just like that, a giant distraction rock crashed into my jar. We are women and we compare ourselves to one another. And if it's not purses or cars, we compare our looks, friends, weight, clothes, personalities, mothering, children, marriages, and many other things. We can find the smallest of things to compare ourselves to other women. While comparison is one of the most common experiences in the history of being women, it plants dangerous seeds of doubt into our spirits.

When your husband's career lands you in the middle of the world of professional athletes, the spirit of competition and comparison is never far away. To make matters worse, the women I am around at the ballpark all seem to be younger, prettier, and wealthier than I am. Suddenly I feel like a pauper among them. Looking at them, I feel as though I lack in every area. They don't make me feel that way; all my thoughts and feelings of inadequacy do.

But you don't have to be surrounded by Major League Baseball wives to feel the effects of comparison. We all compare our lives to others. Each of us may compare differently, but we all compare. I for one size myself up to women who are quiet and calm. I am an outgoing, talkative person who doesn't know how to tone it down when I get filled with joy, excitement, or love for others.

Once in a Bible study group, I expressed my desire to change my personality. One of the quiet women in the group spoke up. "Why would you want to change who God has made you?" Why, indeed? When we voice our comparisons, they are degrading of others and ourselves. God made individuals, each in His image to glorify Him (Genesis 1:27). Who are we to question His work? Yet we do. God does not forget us; He knows us intimately and values us. When we find our worth in the One who created us, accepting the love He has for us, comparisons wane.

After the list of internal distractions formed, I began to look at the external distractions that fill my time. Although these are my own distractions, many woman struggle with the same—or very similar—distractions from their relationship with God.

## SCHEDULE STUFFERS

As I looked over my calendar, I identified the items that were necessary and those that were unnecessary. It allowed me to eliminate the commitments I made because of fear, boredom, lonliness, or an inability to say no.

One of the determining factors in eliminating unnecessary commitments was to look at the activities and rank the stress level each caused me. While some of the events were for great causes, they still caused great stress. I found no joy or peace in the activity. So I finished my commitment and didn't volunteer again.

Another way I eliminated activities was initiated by something my husband said. One night when I was complaining about having too much to do, he very quietly said, "You have the right hand syndrome. When someone asks for a volunteer, your right hand shoots up so quickly no one else gets a chance to volunteer. Your servant's heart is a little too quick to respond."

He was right. I wanted to be helpful, to serve, and to look like the dutiful Christian woman who had it all together and could do it all. When the next opportunity to volunteer arrived, I held my right hand down with my left. I wanted to be helpful, yet I knew I should not choose the battle. Others volunteered, and the events went on without me being overwhelmed.

When we choose activities that glorify God and are not simply schedule stuffers, God will give us the ability, strength, wisdom, patience, joy, and grace to accomplish them.

## RELATIONSHIPS

Our spouse or a member of the opposite sex can be a distraction when their importance is prioritized before God. Our relationships are important. God created us to have relationships—first with Him, then with others. When God is first, He directs us and guides us toward a healthy relationship. In a relationship with a spouse or spouse-to-be, we are called to become one (Genesis 2:24). The distractions begin when a person becomes more important than God. In any relationship, putting God at the center sets you up for a successful connection. Life will not be perfect, but the perfect One is at the center of your relationship.

## FRIENDSHIPS

Friendships can also be a distraction. Some years ago our marriage was going through some tough times. Two girlfriends and I met for lunch once a month. One of them had recently separated from her husband. Let's just say she became a saleswoman for divorce, telling us how great the separation was. She offered advice. "I wouldn't put up with that." "He shouldn't treat you that way." "Leave that loser."

My husband and I had grown apart. We were both at fault and were in a cycle of discontentment. My girlfriends didn't challenge me to work on my marriage. They did not offer to pray redemption over our relationship. They encouraged separation and divorce to teach him a lesson. These were toxic relationships and were not helping save my marriage. My lunch dates ended. Seeking God and a healthy marriage meant reevaluating friendships.

## CHILDREN

Throughout our lives, we go through different seasons of distractions, but parenthood creates a host of new, and often intense, distractions. First, there's the flurry of worrisome thoughts. Then, there's the distraction of busyness. While we're busy taking care of them, we fret over whether or not we're doing anything right, we correct the things we have not done right, and we attempt to keep up with what we think we are supposed to do as parents. All the while being dragged further and further away from God.

Each season of motherhood presents its own concerns. And while being a mother is important, we must remember our Father in heaven loves our children more.

> *Which of you, if your son asks for bread, will give him a stone? Or if he asks for a fish, will give him a snake? If you, then, though you are evil, know how to give good gifts to your children, how much more will your Father in heaven give good gifts to those who ask him!*
>
> —*Matthew 7:9–11*

Giving our children to the Lord is the most difficult part of our parenting experience. They are His. And while we are tasked to guide them on earth, we are not tasked to worry about every aspect of their lives. Once my boys were in college, my mothering duties changed. I had to release them to Jesus completely. We had raised them in a godly home to be successful, independent men. Allowing them to go to college with our love and prayers is our call from God.

## HEALTH/APPEARANCE

Our lives are one big journey of being healthy, struggling to stay healthy, or not caring about being healthy. Even a positive endeavor, like trying to stay healthy, was leading me to distraction. I was consumed with food buying and preparation, working out, and working out more. Don't get me wrong. I work out most every day. Working out clears my head and energizes my body. The distraction begins when the focus of being healthy takes priority over time with God. When my mind starts to wander into the obsession of losing weight or toning up, it takes me away from God's desire for my health and physical appearance.

When allowing food to take an extreme focus in our lives, it becomes an obsession. Excessive focus on what we are going to eat or not eat or how much more we can work out is not concentrating on the health benefits but the obsession. To be spiritually healthy is the foundation for balance in our lives (Romans 8:5–6). Being obedient to God makes room for His Spirit to roam.

## TECHNOLOGY

This category has been the biggest time sucker of all for me recently. Reading emails or blogs and researching information takes me down rabbit holes. Facebook, Twitter, Instagram, or whatever the trending news feed at the time may be, take our attention and cause time-eating distractions. In order to become more aware of when technology consumed my time, one day I started the stopwatch on my phone and opened my laptop.

Even though I knew the timer was running, I soon forgot. I checked my email and read a couple blogs. Then I scrolled through my Twitter feed and checked Facebook. By then I remembered the stopwatch. More than one hour and twenty minutes had passed from the time I opened the computer to the time I remembered the stopwatch. I had wasted way more than an hour. Guilt engulfed me.

But technology wasn't a time sucker alone. When my husband and I planned a weekend trip and left the kids home with a babysitter, I committed to also spending the weekend away from the computer. In order to do this, though, I asked my youngest son to tend to a computer game I was playing online. In the game I had to feed a dog. My son's responsibility was to feed the dog once a day. When I returned and checked my game, the dog had run away—the outcome when you don't feed him. I screamed for my son to come to the computer. When he did, I reprimanded him and sent him to his room. One of the other boys was sitting on the couch and very quietly said, "Mom, you do realize this is a fake dog in an online game?"

I put computer time and games before my children. I also put it before my time with God. The day my timer was set, I had only read one chapter in the Bible. Honestly, Bible time ate into my time and my to-do lists. (You know how I love lists!) I was prioritizing technology over the righteous pursuit of God. We must discipline ourselves to intentionally set time aside for pursuing God. To do this, structuring allotted time periods for lingering on the web is a must in order to achieve balance.

## SPORTING EVENTS

I am often asked if I enjoy baseball. More than 30 years of professional baseball and raising three boys who were on the field at every opportunity, you would hope there was some enjoyment. I have always loved baseball, not just because I married a baseball guy—but maybe I am married to a baseball guy because of my love of baseball. As a young teenager, my mother would take me to the local ballpark and leave me to watch games. I could spend hours watching the game and still do. Now, baseball is an everyday constant in my life. However, the distractions come late in the baseball season.

Each September, my husband's team is usually fighting for a playoff spot, and my competitive side kicks in. I intensely watch every pitch, every hit, and every ball fielded or caught. In the fall, this is the king of distractions for me. I look at stats of other teams, watch SportsCenter and MLB Network for hours, and constantly think and talk about baseball. It becomes a bigger distraction for my husband because he cannot get away from it even for a minute. My life becomes consumed, and I become spiritually drained.

Being aware of this weakness allows me to make better decisions. I have to prioritize my quiet time with God by setting aside time each morning to read my Bible and choosing to stop throughout the day to pray for His will— not mine—to come.

## READING

When my children were small, they learned the word *neglect*. It was in direct response to me lying in bed or on the couch with a book. I can lose hours in the pages of a book—even one I've read before!

Prioritizing time spent in God's Word should be the goal. Keeping God's Word active in our lives helps us to remember not to allow these distractions to become our priority. Even though I love to read, I can be distracted by a story in a novel before being engulfed in the stories of the Bible. Priority is the key.

## LACK OF REST

Downtime is not the same as it was in years past. Because we can be immediately alerted to every text, email, and social media notification, we can often feel we have to in turn immediately respond to the dings, pings, and vibrations. And if we aren't responding to the endless barrage of others' messages, we're busy documenting our own lives to upload to social media. It adds to the busy state of our daily lives and takes away from time to rest.

Sabbath rest is a day of rest or worship. No work must take place on the Sabbath, as is recognized by the Christian and Jewish church. How many of us relax on Sunday after a day of worship? Not many from the people I have asked. We leave church and run errands or shop for our weekly groceries. We go home and cook lunch, clean the house, or do laundry. Rather than giving us rest from our previous week, Sundays start our week.

Through our belief in the death and Resurrection of Christ, we are given eternal rest. Jesus called those who were weary, all of us, to come to Him. He would give us rest. Coming to Him, Jesus restores our communion with Him. Restlessness happens in our busy lives. We have rest in Jesus.

At the end of Luke 10, we read about Mary and Martha. They were the sisters of Lazarus, a personal friend of Jesus. They lived in Bethany, a town where Jesus and His disciples visited. Martha opened her home to them. As she busied herself preparing food for the group, Martha became frustrated because her sister Mary sat at Jesus' feet listening to what He said.

Let's just say Martha is my kind of girl. I'll bet she made a list of things she needed to do as soon as Jesus walked through her door. *Hey, Jesus is coming to lunch. Give me a five-subject, college-ruled notebook, some sticky notes, and a box of pens. I have lists to make!*

Frustration can definitely happen if 13 people walked in and needed dinner, but your sister is sitting there doing *nothing.* Martha told Jesus what she thought He should do. "Tell her to help me!" (v. 40).

In our busy lives, we tell Jesus the same types of things. *Take this burden from me. Jesus, take care of this storm in my life. Find me a parking space close to the door because of the rain. Help me get all of my tasks done. Quick.* We tell Him to care for us because we are too busy to waste time on such things. He loves us and answers our prayers, but should we be praying for these things or focus on praying for His presence?

Jesus responded by telling Martha she was worried about many things that didn't matter. Only one thing was needed—Him (vv. 41–42). Mary had chosen to sit at His feet and learn. It wasn't about her position in the room but the position of her heart. She was aware of what He wanted to teach her. Martha was distracted in her busyness. It wasn't that Martha was working too hard or doing too much, it was that she was not focused on what was important in that moment—learning from Jesus.

Martha was a devout follower of Christ, inviting Him into her home to serve Him. She let her list of to-dos take her from His presence even though He was with her. She didn't notice Him or what He wanted to teach her. She was not necessarily consumed by sin; she was consumed by distractions. Don't we find ourselves in the same position? How often do I think I need to respond to an email, take a call, read an article, or feed a fake dog before I connect with Him?

We can sit at the feet of Jesus while praying, cooking, cleaning, checking emails, working, bartering with the kids, or talking with friends. Asking Jesus to be our teacher and companion during these activities places our hearts in a position to live in His presence and seek to learn.

I submitted these lists of internal and external distractions to God and asked Him which to delete.

Take some time to refine the list for yourself and ask God to prioritize it. Each of our lists is different, but the importance of God is the same. Be with Him in what you are doing. Making God your priority, place Him in the center of your life and give Him permission to have control of your distractions. Then put the list aside and sit at the feet of Jesus without any distractions.

What a mighty God we serve. Let's continue to pray the distractions of this life do not overpower His mighty power. We may not always be distraction free, but being aware of what distracts us allows us to open our spirit for God to dwell. Stay present in His presence.

# Spiritual Attack and Ringing

## CHAPTER THREE

Be aware! When you are going through a period of learning God's Word and growing closer to Him, be prepared for attacks that pull you further away from His Spirit. Fear of attacks is an area where I struggle. We don't want to be attacked by the enemy, but we don't always get what we want when we are seeking a closer relationship with God. These tests are to be expected and used as an opportunity to prevail and reveal God's glory.

Sometimes I feel as though the more I do in His name, the more obstacles and attacks I encounter. The enemy wants to takes us down so that God will not be glorified. When we are a mouthpiece for the Holy One, we are a threat to evil. "For our struggle is not against flesh and blood, but against the rulers, against the authorities, against the powers of this dark world and against the spiritual forces of evil in the heavenly realms" (Ephesians 6:12).

Seeking a deeper connection to Christ seemed to open a door for the attacks to begin within me. I let the negative words replay in my mind—the "I can't" thoughts, the confusion about whether I was truly hearing God's guidance, and the questions of whether or not the journey was important. Over and over I doubted the process. I became hostile and argumentative with my husband and children.

The enemy presented himself as fierce anger boiling deep inside my mind. And I kept it to myself way too long.

The attacks continued. I questioned the value of confiding in others about the negativity and doubt I was experiencing. I was scared to be vulnerable about my struggles. And I had forgotten Peter's advice:

> *Dear friends, do not be surprised at the fiery ordeal that has come on you to test you, as though something strange were happening to you. But rejoice inasmuch as you participate in the sufferings of Christ, so that you may be overjoyed when his glory is revealed.*
>
> *—1 Peter 4:12–13*

Sharing how and when we are attacked or tempted is intimidating. It requires vulnerability and honesty with others, God, and ourselves. If we admit to the attacks from the devil, our imperfections and weaknesses are exposed. And we may be further attacked if others respond with judgment. But only concerning ourselves with the potential judgment of others will stagnate our lives and faith. We hinder God's movement within us.

The honesty in our spirits uncovers past hurts, hang-ups, and hardships long buried in an effort to avoid dealing with them. Breathe deep the Spirit of God. Rely on His Spirit to guide you. His Spirit has the power to cleanse. Stop walking around with the clutter of the past.

Uncovering junk in my mind and spirit revealed what I was attempting to hide from God, hoping it would never be revealed. It is a deception to believe we can hide anything from God. He is all-knowing. Though we may be glad people can't see the temptations we keep our minds, He knows.

When I think my comfortable Christian world is the place I want to linger, God shows me it is not where He wants me to stay. Satan shows me he wants to keep me where negativity and doubt infect my soul. Satan is real. He will use all of our hurts to hurt us more. He will use our hang-ups to hang us and hardships to make life harder. Each of the places I feel I have under control is fair game. When we are glorifying God in the mightiest way, the enemy wants to attack. Be aware.

On an early morning after a late-night game, my husband Dave and I walked to a baseball outreach at an inner-city sports ministry for underprivileged urban kids The Lord had been nagging me. I know He doesn't nag, but it sometimes feels that way when I don't want to be obedient. He had been encouraging me to write about marriage. Our story is one of healing and transformation, a story that has been helpful to many couples. We have led marriage courses, spoken at events, and counseled couples together. And each time we made waves of positive marriage impact, our relationship came under attack. The attacks are not all the same, but they have the same effect: a storm. Stormy times in our marriage inevitably pull us away from each other and God. Satan attacks to stop us from making a spiritual difference in marriages and glorifying God. So I worried writing about marriage would cause another storm. I wanted nothing to do with another storm. At the time our marriage was stronger than ever, and we were focused on God. Why would I want to rock a steady boat?

But as we walked to the outreach game that day, the nudge became stronger. Finally, I told Dave that God was calling me to write about marriage and I did *not* want to obey. He stayed quiet for a couple of minutes. Then, in the middle of a crosswalk, he turned to me, "God can do this. He can protect us from the attack. You have to obey God if you know this call is from Him. We will pray together every day and seek His guidance."

Did he have to make it sound so easy? Why did my husband want us to come under attack? I immediately stopped and screamed an exuberant, "What? Seriously?" He gently took my arm and guided me safely to the sidewalk. At that moment, I knew obedience to God was needed.

No matter what attacks the enemy would assault us with, we would be strong together. The story needed to be told. With God's healing, I had a secure and supportive marriage. We had come so far since our tenth year of marriage, when our intense self-focus had turned us away from each other. We worked hard together to get to a place where our relationship was healed and transformed. Supported by God and my husband, I couldn't keep God's healing to myself.

Within hours of penning the first blog about marriage, the attacks began. My husband made a comment; I snapped back. We walked to separate rooms. Doors slammed. Hurt and anger resided where we were determined it would not be. A deep breath, a call out to Jesus, a prayer prayed. We entered the living room at the same time. Locking hands, we prayed. Attacks are inevitable. Defeat is optional.

I chose defeat at that moment. I put writing about marriage on hold. It was an attack that took me to a place of fear. Satan uses fear to stop us. He uses many temptations to keep us stuck.

As Christians, we are not exempt from attacks. The devil tempted Jesus. Jesus came from Galilee to the Jordan River to be baptized by John—a moment that marked the beginning of His ministry. With baptism, Jesus publicly identified with our human weakness. He was confirmed by John as the Messiah. After He ascended the water, the heavens immediately opened. He was filled with the Holy Spirit equipping Him for His work as the Messiah. His mighty work was beginning (Matthew 3:13–17).

Soon after, Jesus was led by the Holy Spirit into the desert to be attacked by the devil. Jesus went from the spiritual high of baptism and being filled by the Holy Spirit to a spiritual low of attack by the devil. The same can happen to us. While in the wilderness, before being attacked by the devil, Jesus fasted for 40 days and 40 nights. He was hungry when Satan approached Him. The attack began.

The first temptation was to make Jesus question God's providence. Satan didn't try to denounce Jesus' Sonship proclaimed at His baptism. He urged Jesus to use His power to meet His needs. Jesus responded with Scripture, insisting spiritual nourishment is more significant than physical.

Satan was offering Jesus the one thing that would take away His physical hunger. Jesus could turn the rock into bread, eat, and not be hungry. But the bread would only bring momentary satisfaction to His stomach. The Word of God is not a momentary satisfaction but eternal sustenance for our souls. Relying on God provides nourishment for life and eternity. "Jesus answered . . . 'Man shall not live on bread alone, but on every word that comes from the mouth of God'" (Matthew 4:4).

In the second temptation, Satan tried to twist Scripture by asking Jesus to tempt faith. It was to tempt Christ to take a stand as God, giving glory and celebrity to Himself. It was to gain recognition. Jesus trusted God and did not need to test Him. He knew God protected Him.

Satan attacks when we are in need. He tempts us to step out of God's Word and rely on our strength to support us through the struggle. "I can do it myself," becomes our motto instead of relying on God or digging deep into Scripture to find our strength.

The third and final temptation was the possibility to seize a kingdom and avoid the Cross. Jesus could avoid the struggles and pain He would endure. Jesus continued to show His allegiance to God. Taking our focus from God in momentary fulfillment displaces our worship of God and His glory.

Satan wants to take away any mission that will give God glory. If he had taken away the mission of Jesus, there would be no eternal life, no forgiveness of sins, and no peace that transcends all understanding (see Philippians 4:7). The same is true in our lives. God has called us to make a difference for His kingdom. If we do not prepare our souls for the opportunity to make a difference, what will happen? We will not fulfill His plan.

Jesus commanded Satan to leave. After Satan left, angels attended to Jesus. They provided care to strengthen Him and prepare Him for the ministry ahead.

Being the Son of God did not mean Jesus was exempt from attacks. Jesus lived life on earth and was surrounded by attacks, but He stood firm on His Father's calling.

Like Jesus, we can also command Satan to leave. And God can minister to our souls and prepare us for what He wants to do in and through us.

This preparation of our spirits helps to avoid destruction. Spiritual nourishment, trusting God, and allegiance to God is the recipe for surviving attack. Jesus' temptation in the wilderness is a source of encouragement and instruction for us. His example is helpful to us when fighting attacks.

Be the woman who, when your feet hit the floor each morning, the devil knows he cannot waver your strong faith. When we expect attacks, and we prepare by being confident and knowledgeable in God's Word, we don't have to live in fear. He is with us through it all.

*Be strong and courageous. Do not be afraid or terrified because of them, for the Lord your God goes with you; he will never leave you nor forsake you.*

*—Deuteronomy 31:6*

Reading God's Word is vital not because it's something we have to do—another item to add to our checklist—but because it is our best resource to get to know Him better. Our strength in avoiding temptation is directly linked to reading the Word. There are numerous Bible-reading plans. You can read the Bible in six months, one year, or two years. You can read book by book, chronologically, or by starting with the Gospels. But the best way to read the Bible is to *open it!* Get in the habit of opening your Bible every day. Plans are great if you don't feel guilty or like a failure when you don't follow the plan completely. Perfection isn't key here. Just start somewhere.

Trusting God to be there gives us strength to deter the attacks. Strong spirits stand sturdy when attacked. Trust believes something is reliable, good, honest, and efficient. God is all of that and more. When we know God is our protector, and He will take care of us in all circumstances, our strength is fortified. We can trust Him to be with us during all attacks.

Like a mountain lion hunting down the weakest prey, the enemy looks for places of vulnerability to separate you from God (1 Peter 5:8). The root of his ability is unbelief, making us doubt our allegiance to God. No matter how strong we are in our walk with Christ, we all struggle with doubt.

In Mark 9:14–27, we read the story of a man who brought his son to be healed by Jesus. The man believed in the power of Jesus' healings so much he brought his son to Him, yet the man said to Jesus, "but if you can do anything" (v. 22). Who brings their son to Jesus knowing the miracles He has done and says, "if You can"? Me. I bring so much to Jesus, asking Him, "if You can." If You can heal. If You can help. If You can hear. If You can, Jesus. Questioning if God can work in and through us, even though we believe in the one true God.

Jesus replied, "'If you can'? . . . Everything is possible for one who believes" (v. 23). At this, the boy's father exclaimed, "I do believe; help me overcome my unbelief!" (v. 24). The father believed in the miracles of Jesus. However, he admitted his time of unbelief. Admitting times of unbelief and asking God to help us overcome those times is transformational in our strength to overcome spiritual attacks.

In this journey of seeking God's desire for far more than we could ask or imagine, we need to recognize His almighty power in these vulnerable times. His power stops the enemy's hold of my doubts. Admitting we will have moments of doubt allows our spirits to know we can still believe during our unbelief. We can thwart the attacks, not in our strength but by His.

One particular area the enemy likes to attack me personally is in my mothering skills (or lack thereof). Going through the process of determining what God desires to do in my life brought on an onslaught of attack. My history of little confidence and big doubts led me to question whether or not I was worthy of raising my boys.

In an age when society encourages (often rightfully so!) female independence and lack of dependence on a man, I felt drawn to another path. I got rid of the hyphen in my name and took on the fullness of being my husband's wife and my sons' mother. My husband's job takes him away the majority of eight months a year. I knew God was asking me to quit my job as an intensive care nurse and stay home with my boys and be the stabilizing factor in our chaotic baseball life. I was going against the current belief that "strong women can do it all." I had to be stronger than "a woman who can do it all" by doing what was right for my family.

My new title became "family manager" while my husband pursued his career. My vulnerability came in the form of submission to my husband and children. This was not subservience. *It was service.* I didn't want to give up or give in. I wanted to serve my family by giving my all to them.

In my nursing job, I was in control. If someone was in critical condition, there were procedures to stabilize him or her if at all possible. I had been trained to be a successful nurse. Not every medical situation could be corrected. In situations when the outcome was not positive, there were often proven reasons why a patient didn't survive. But there were no procedures for being a successful mother in my textbooks.

I was told many times when I was younger that I would not be a good mother. People said I wasn't good with kids. I believed it. And this lie played over and over again in my mind. The message became my own. I am not sure why people spoke those words to me, but I embraced them. I became self-focused, deciding I should seek a nursing career in the military. Traveling the world was my new dream. Marriage and children were the last things on my mind. A road map to my particular vulnerabilities was created by the enemy well before children came into my life.

When my husband entered my life, all of my carefully laid out plans began to tumble. When we started to talk about marriage, the idea of children followed closely behind. Without a doubt, I knew we would have babies . . . and many of them! Funny how when God's plans fall into place they disrupt the plans you lay. From the beginning, the enemy grasped my fears and strangled my joy. Even during pregnancy, the fear of failure impaled my thoughts. How could having kids be smart? I would never be a good mother. Three wonderful gifts from God, gifts that are not easy to raise, even without the fear of failure. The enemy knew he had me from the beginning.

Our eldest child is a brilliant and strong-willed young man. At an early age, he was a believing Christian, baptized at 14 years old. Then something went wrong; he began to slip away. I blamed others who came along in his life—an atheist girlfriend, a philosophy professor, graduate school, and liberal-minded friends—for the path paved away from his beliefs about a loving God. The anger I had toward these people and situations became consuming. Then I began to look at the one and only enemy to be blamed—the devil. The enemy attacked my son where he knew he could and continued to dig and dig until my son began to reject the family who loves him and the God who loves him even more. As my son pushed away from the family, the enemy began attacking me.

Each hurtful word between my son and me took me to a deeper, darker place far from the Lord. The tape replayed, and the fear returned to reinforce the words, the lie, making it seem like truth. *I will never be a good mother!* I began to blame only myself; I was so distraught with my list of wrongs as a parent that I became separated from God's direction. I even questioned God's love for me. How could He love me if I failed at the one job He had entrusted to me?

During this time, I was asked to speak at a conference. As I stood in front of a room full of baseball wives and girlfriends, my heart raced and my head spun. How could I speak to these women about God when I was feeling so distant from Him? This spiritual journey of growing deeper with Christ was failing terribly. The child God had given me to raise for Him was stepping further away from his beliefs. If I couldn't guide my children in their faith, how on earth could I speak to these women? I wanted to run.

My notes slipped out of my numb fingers. Bending to pick them up, I heard a small whisper, "You can't even hold on to your faith. Who are you to speak?" I took a deep breath and leaned on a stool behind me. Embarrassment is the only thing that kept me in front of these women. The talk was titled "The Normal Life." I started with, "Throughout life, we will face challenges, trials, and triumphs, and through them all, we have a chance to have an encounter with God. The Normal Life is one that worships Christ, one where our circumstances, challenges, and trials are an opportunity to worship and glorify God." I remember nothing after. God took over. He used me while I was under attack. God used me to glorify His Word.

I failed in many situations. I would yell at my children—absolutely losing it at times. I didn't always give good advice, and I wasn't always a great role model. I have asked for forgiveness from my boys, my husband, and Jesus many times for my mistakes. When these attacks come from the enemy during times of getting closer to the Lord, we have to stand strong in the promise that God is with us. In the anticipation of these attacks, we remain determined. We cling to His Word.

We have to make sure our spirit is ready for God's Spirit to move, even under attack. To allow God's Spirit to move more freely, we need to clean out the clutter that grows within us. After evaluating our hearts and identifying the distractions, we are ready to clean out all the stagnant areas and purify ourselves from everything that contaminates body and spirit.

> *Therefore, since we have these promises, dear friends, let us purify ourselves from everything that contaminates body and spirit, perfecting holiness out of reverence for God.*
> *—2 Corinthians 7:1*

What a profound calling. Is it even possible? As I analyzed my spiritual life, I identified many hurts, hang-ups, and hardships that I allowed to inhabit the deepest parts of my soul. Like many of us, I would revisit the familiar ones over and over again. Comfort resides in the normalcy of the clutter inhabiting our spirits. Cluttered areas are where the enemy takes deep hold and attacks easily.

We don't like looking at the ugly parts of our lives. Cleaning these areas is not easy. Pride supersedes humbleness. When we assess the areas needed to purify our spirit from everything that contaminates, it reveals a need for a spiritual rinsing. We have to rinse the crevices of our soul. The deeper I looked in my spirit, the more apparent the need became. I actually needed a spiritual cleansing with a commercial-sized power washer that gets deep into the crevices. Our souls need scrubbing even if we don't want to, even if it makes us uncomfortable.

Life was comfortable and happy. Great things were happening in my husband's career and my children's lives, even though there were bumps along the way. One season of life was changing into another. Empty nest was looming large. My three boys were happy and thriving. I would be spending more time with my husband. Why would I want to rock a very steady emotional boat to dig deep and uncover hurts, hang-ups, and hardships I didn't want to discover? Why would I want to dig deeper when more attacks were imminent? We choose to go through a spiritual cleansing because we want to have a deeper connection with Christ, allowing His Spirit to move more freely in and through us.

*And God is able to bless you abundantly, so that in all things at all times, having all that your need, you will abound in every good work.*
*—2 Corinthians 9:8*

This deeper connection happens when we become transparent and honest. Looking into the crevices isn't always comfortable, but it does begin the process of spiritual cleansing. Identifying the clutter in our spirits is the first step. Knowing the condition of our spirits and understanding the distractions that pull us away from time with God prepares us for the attacks to come. Name the distractions and hang-ups. I wrote them in my journal. Writing them down began to release their power over me.

This time, I didn't burn the list. I kept it. Not to hold on to the burdens, but to be reminded of the healing power of the spiritual rinsing God was providing. I could revisit the list later and give a praise report of the power of God through the cleansing of my spirit. *Lord, make a difference in me so I can make a difference for You.*

I reluctantly began the power washing of my spirit. It took time to uncover all God wanted to reveal in preparation for Him to do far more than I could imagine, guess, or request. All according to His power that is at work in us. Thankfully, it's not up to what we can do. He works within us to bring about His glory. Cleansing us from the distractions, lies, and sin in our lives brings our spirits to a place for Him to work.

This is work we all need to do because sin lives within all of us. While we are spiritually cleansed when we give our lives to Christ, each day we find things that cause us to defy Christ's continual cleansing. Confessing whatever sin may be alive in your spirit then releasing it to God by asking for forgiveness cleanses our spirit. We may not believe sin is in our lives, but it is. We just don't want to uncover it and reveal it. Sin is alive, and, unrepented, it weighs us down and keeps us from being all we can be with Christ. We don't always identify some patterns in our lives as sin. When we worry and fear, we sin. God commands us to not worry about tomorrow and to fear not. We sin when we dwell there.

The attacks will come when we start uncovering sin because Satan knows uncovering and repenting of sin draws us closer to God. In being close to God, we can glorify Him in a more powerful way. His power lives inside us. Relinquishing sin gives the Holy Spirit more power to release faith and boldness within us.

God is faithful. He is with us through the attacks and the cleansing of our spirits. Our body is the temple of God's Spirit. When we ask Him to create a clean heart and renew a right spirit within us, we are ready for His Spirit to roam freely. Changes happen as we cleanse our spirit.

Make a change. It could be directional, emotional, physical, or spiritual. Uncovering the changes we need to make to create free space in our spirits for the Holy Spirit to roam is the rinsing needed. Change comes with obedience. Obey God by allowing the change within our spirits and outwardly in our actions. We are already clean because of God's Word. To keep our spirit clean we need to obey it.

With spiritual cleansing comes a divine nature within us. Our souls are purified and an overwhelming power happens in a spiritual rinsing. The rinsing feels like a spiritual power washing where hurts, hang-ups, and hardships are more deep-seeded than others. Some distractions set in deeper than others. A few distractions aren't revealed at first and only rise to the surface with the continued power washing into the painful expanse of our heart. The rinsing is continual. We have to make sure we don't let the distractions return and set into the walls of our hearts again. We may need to add a little bleach to the water!

Even now I am under attack. The doubt and negative thoughts come back. But we stand strong in God's strength when we pray, release the pain, speak His Word, and grasp the love He gives. Knowing we are children of God and He has good works for us to do is a continual rinse to our spirits. Continuing to evaluate our hearts and expose the distractions keeps us in the fight for the prize—the prize of joy and peace and good works for God.

*For we are God's handiwork, created in Christ Jesus to do good works, which God prepared in advance for us to do.*

*—Ephesians 2:10*

Walking through this spiritual rinsing can become lonely at times. During our spiritual journey, we know we need to cling to Jesus, and we need to take steps to hold ourselves accountable.

## WE NEED A FRIEND

Having a trusted Christian friend to keep us on a biblical track is essential. A friend to pray with, be transparent and vulnerable with, and cry or scream with is a blessing beyond belief. If you do not have someone in your life, pray about finding someone. Begin at church, in Bible studies, in outreach programs. Seek them out. Then ask. Ask them to lunch or coffee. Share the experience we are having in searching for God's desires for our lives and travel the journey together. Get to know them. Transparency will come. Build a relationship of trust and honesty. It takes time but is worth the investment. Invest in each other during this experience.

## WE NEED TO JOURNAL

Find some paper, a notebook, or journal, and write down your thoughts. Write down the distractions keeping you separated from God. Writing them down brings them into the light and is the first step in healing. When acknowledged, the distractions lose the power they had in darkness. Nothing is too trivial or too minor; write down anything keeping you from the transformation God wants.

## WE NEED TO DIG DEEP

Evaluate the dark places of your heart. Dig deep. Be aware of the attacks. Take the power washer and rinse out all the deep dark crevices in the stagnant areas of your spirit. "Being confident of this, that he who began a good work in you will carry it on to completion until the day of Christ Jesus" (Philippians 1:6).

## WE NEED TO LET GO OF CONTROL AND FEAR

Throughout the transformational journey, you may still experience fear and anxiety. Let's let go of our need to control and together grasp onto the loving hand of the Almighty God. He is with us. I am with you, continuing in the process even knowing the attacks will come. Return to the cleansing of our spirits daily. Uncover the stagnation, power wash it clean, live in the power of His spirit. Together we can go through the spiritual rinsing needed on a continual basis. Determine to trust in God, submit all to Him, and lean on His strength as we move into the work He wants to do in us.

There will be spiritual attacks and struggles every day until the return of Jesus. We have to continue to fight as strong soldiers of Christ, glorifying Him in every victory and thanking Him throughout it all. Don't bring more attention to the enemy; focus on God and what He is doing in your life. Making room in our souls increases the power God infuses us with in our daily lives.

PART 2 |  Discovering the Work God Wants to Do in Us

# *Awareness*

## CHAPTER FOUR

In high school, my best friend and I hung out with a couple of guys from a neighboring town—not the kind of boys you take home to Mama. They were older and liked to have too much fun for Mama's taste. Their request for us to come with them to see their friend seemed like a typical, Wednesday night ride until they mentioned they were meeting him at church. My girlfriend and I snuck a glance at one another, not too sure about the idea. But how big of a drag could it be? We would meet their friend, hang out for a while, and leave for our usual shenanigans. Once in the church, we slithered into the second-to-last row as worship was well underway.

It was the kind of church where worshippers raised their hands, danced, and shouted. The style was much different from the reverent, quiet, hymnal-singing church I grew up in, and it was a world away from my friend's experience of no church at all. We sat snickering as hairpins flew out of the tightly wound buns of the church ladies who threw their arms high shouting, "Halleluiah!" and, "Praise the Lord!"

A man jumped up behind the pulpit as the music slowed, and he prayed like I had never heard. He spoke to Jesus as if he were speaking to a friend. I shifted nervously in my seat. My heart beat so forcefully, I thought for sure my chest was visibly pounding through my shirt. *Did he say a relationship with Jesus?* I didn't know what it meant, but I was intrigued.

After the service, the guy our friends knew approached us. He thanked us profusely for staying for the service. Then he asked, "What did you think?" I smiled but thought, *This will be the last time I come to a crazy place like this.* He excitedly invited us to return the next week. Later my friend and I agreed never to return.

But the following Wednesday night we once again slipped into the second-to-last row. My thoughts were the same as the week before as I watched it all unfold again. Then back on Sunday night. And Wednesday. Why did we return again and again? The guys we first came with had lost interest. Was it the magnetic feeling that drew us back? Or was it because I begged my best friend to go because I "liked" the music? Whatever it was, I kept going.

During these visits, the pastor asked if anyone wanted to give their lives to the Lord. I felt as though someone were pushing me to the front of the church. I turned, no one was there. Another service, another request, another urging. I was 16 and clueless about the whole God thing. I was not aware of how His presence, His Spirit, could urge someone quietly in his or her heart. I did know that everything in me wanted to go forward that night . . . and the next.

Finally, God won. I walked forward, one slow step at a time, and wholeheartedly gave my heart to the Lord. His presence was so powerful and real; I could feel His Spirit fill me. Peace overcame me like I had never felt before. My life took on newness in the awareness of Him. Leaving church, floating on a cloud, I was convinced this feeling would last. I was a new creation. I was forgiven.

Then life happened. Bit by bit, my awareness of God was chipped away by the circumstances of life. Life didn't go the peaceful way I thought it would once I had Jesus in my heart. So I distanced myself from God. I stopped going to church and reading my Bible. I made bad choices and went back to living according to my power and control. I thought I was in control of my chaotic life. Time trickled on and before I knew it I was in college, and then out of college. And God became more and more distant. Where was He? Why did I no longer feel He was there?

When the struggles and complexities of life happen, we tend to forget that God is with us. Always. It's easy to become consumed with the moment we are living, rather than His presence. Circumstances in our immediate sight become our focus. Doubt and fear overwhelm us and make us give up on the things we cannot see.

All these experiences rob us of the Lord's presence that remains within us. At the beginning of the Bible, we see how anger and sin separate us from the Holy Spirit. Genesis 4 tells the story of Cain and Abel. These two brothers each brought their own offering to the Lord. Abel brought a generous offering. Cain's was thoughtless and careless. So Cain became angry and jealous when God showed favor to Abel.

Cain threw a tantrum and pouted. He chose to position himself away from God's presence. Full of anger, Cain fought his brother and killed him. When God asked Cain where his brother was, Cain lied. He lied to God even though he stood directly in His presence. God knew. He knew about the murder. God knew where Abel died. He gave Cain a chance to draw close to Him, even after Cain's jealousy, anger, self-seeking, lying, and murderous behavior. But Cain did not humble himself before God, so God punished him. Cain could no longer till the ground productively, and he became a wandering vagabond.

*Cain said to the Lord, "My punishment is more than I can bear. Today you are driving me from the land, and I will be hidden from your presence; I will be a restless wanderer on the earth, and whoever finds me will kill me."*

*—Genesis 4:13–14*

Cain spoke his dismay and fear of being murdered by the avengers of Abel's murder. Cain was separated from God, but God's protection continued to be with Cain. God placed a mark on him to protect him from harm.

As believing Christians, we know God promises to be with us always; He will never leave us. We know He numbers every hair on our heads, and He knew us before we were created in our mother's womb (Jeremiah 1:5). So what happens when what we know and what we feel don't connect?

I knew I had lost the awareness of Christ in my life. So I recommitted my life to Christ and felt more aware of His presence than I ever had. Busyness had taken over the awareness of God.

We all feel disconnected at times. We often spend too much time trying to understand where we belong, where we should be, and what we should be doing. You are not alone. The feeling of being disconnected happens. We get busy. We don't want to hear the answers God desires to give us. We try to do life on our own. We get distracted.

Once we are forgiven of sin and are in a committed relationship with Christ, we will never be truly disconnected from Him, no matter the distractions, doubts, or fears. Our faith is a journey, continually growing, learning, and changing.

Our journey is repeatedly developing a deeper awareness of Christ's Spirit within us. Allowing His Spirit to fill the exposed spaces in our souls, our spirits become alive and awake with the understanding of His presence.

When we feel distracted or separated from Him, we first need to determine whether or not Jesus is truly our Savior. Have we placed a different savior in front of Him? Identifying the idols that have blocked our awareness of God is the beginning. Defining Jesus as our Savior defines who we are in Him.

*The LORD is my rock, my fortress and my deliverer; my God is my rock, in whom I take refuge, my shield and the horn of my salvation, my stronghold.*

*—Psalm 18:2*

The confidence that Jesus is our Savior lays the foundation of our relationship with Him. If we place anything in a more critical position than Christ, we lessen our connection with Him.

Jesus stands with open arms to receive us. He wants to be in a relationship with us. "In him and through faith in him we may approach God with freedom and confidence" (Ephesians 3:12). We can go to God knowing He is anxious to embrace us—just as we are.

Being aware of what keeps us from the understanding of who He is and what He desires develops our attachment to Him. We cannot be satisfied as Christians without our connection to Jesus. Opening our spirits to receive the Holy Spirit's free movement within us creates a battle between the newness of life we receive in Christ and the old longings of our flesh. We have to recondition our souls to permit the reality of who God is, allowing the living Spirit to roam freely within us.

Who is God to us? How do we define Him? God is love. "Whoever does not love does not know God, because God is love" (1 John 4:8). Can we even comprehend the type of love that God offers us? He gives us unconditional, forgiving, freely giving, without-expecting-anything-in-return love?

God's love isn't based on emotion or any human sensation. He doesn't stop loving us because His feelings get hurt, He feels neglected, or we want to do everything our way. His love is enduring and constant. God showed His love in a most defining way. "For God so loved the world that he gave his one and only Son, that whoever believes in him shall not perish but have eternal life" (John 3:16).

He loved His children so much, even in the midst of our sin, abandonment, worship of idols, murder, adultery, and all other sins, He still sacrificed His Son for us. He knew we could never be perfect. Jesus was. That is the love we may never fully comprehend but must embrace.

God refers to us as His beloved. "Put on then, as God's chosen ones, holy and beloved, compassionate hearts, kindness, humility, meekness, and patience" (Colossians 3:12 ESV). His beloved. His love cannot be superseded by any other feeling we could ever have or by any love that any human could feel for us. No other love is possible. We often forget the deep passion Jesus showed for us on the Cross and the same love He extends to us each and every moment.

Sometimes I don't perceive God's love while I'm receiving it. It's in the moments when I look back on situations when I see His love so clearly. The friends who took my best friend and me to church with them had a lot of brokenness in their lives. God loved me so much He guided me to Him even in the chaos of those misguided friends. He saved me. I was not only saved on the altar steps of that church, but God saved me from trouble that could have altered my future. I have many stories of God loving me more than I loved Him or myself—as He always does! His protection for me, his daughter, is overwhelming when I reflect on my life.

Then the distractions of life interfere. Things don't go our way, and we forget. Busy schedules consume us. We sin, and we forget. Being aware of God in our lives is a connection to the love God shows us even when we don't feel it. His presence engulfs our whole being while in communion with Him. Nothing can ultimately separate us from His love when we have committed our lives to Him, but we can distance ourselves from Him with poor choices. Choosing each day to be the best we can be, according to His power, keeps us united with Him and His love.

God is eternal. "Do you not know? Have you not heard? The LORD is the everlasting God, the Creator of the ends of the earth. He will not grow tired or weary, and his understanding no one can fathom" (Isaiah 40:28). God is a constant. He is and will always be. He has no end. In Revelation 22:13, God identifies Himself as the Alpha and the Omega. Alpha and Omega are the first and last letters of the Greek alphabet. He is speaking of His existence as the beginning and the end. Everything began with Him, and it will end with Him. He fills us with His Spirit. God will be our source of life forever. Because He is the end, our eternity lies with Him.

We were created by Him and in His likeness. We are set apart as believers. "To those who by persistence in doing good seek glory, honor and immortality, he will give eternal life" (Roman 2:7). This Scripture truth is a huge concept—sometimes I just cannot wrap my limited mind around it. Wow! I cannot grasp it because I size His existence up to what I know on earth. Nothing lasts forever. Friendships. Jobs. Feelings. Desires. Lives. Everything has an expiration date. I cannot grasp it because I try to understand it in my abilities, not the abilities of an all-powerful God. Clinging to who He is, rather than what we know of earthly value, brings an awareness of His Holy Spirit.

God is forgiving. "I, even I, am he who blots out your transgressions, for my own sake, and remembers your sins no more" (Isaiah 43:25). Better yet, He also forgets all our past problems and mistakes and lets us start over again. The problem begins when we don't forget and start new. He forgets our past mistakes. We must do the same. We are a new creation because of His forgiveness. We only have to ask for His forgiveness.

Our awareness of God's presence heightens the recognition of our sin. Our issues become more apparent. We have a continual choice to focus on our hang-ups, hurts, and hardships or to concentrate on the forgiveness of Christ. Fixating on our circumstances devalues the significance of what Christ sacrificed on the Cross. When we choose to gaze at the sacrifice of Christ, we choose well.

As I grew more aware of God in my spirit, I also became more aware of the layers of the continued buildup of junk in my soul. Not only was I aware of His presence but also of the debris I had piled up. I was able to grasp the busyness and distractions before they took deep root. A continual awareness is necessary.

The Holy Spirit is our daily guide. He guides us into the truth and the plan He has for us. Jesus lights our way, helping us understand the path where He wants us to go. Cling to Him, our lifeline, as He guides us through the plan He has for our lives. God is everywhere at all times and wants to lead us forward. Jesus may not light the path in a way that gives us the comfort of full sight, but He is there. Step out in faith, and let Jesus guide you.

Often when we slip up, make a mistake, or act in a way that is not perfect in our eyes we mentally create a barrier. We're disappointed we didn't act or speak correctly, and instead of relying on His power within us, we become afraid or frustrated. Let Him help you. The walls only divide your spiritual connection with Jesus. This division is self-made.

No matter our mishaps, God continues to be present and guide us in the plan He has for us. Relying on His guidance is a mental and spiritual activity based on trust. When we feel alone, or God's presence feels minimal, we have to concentrate on God's Spirit. Trusting God and the power He possesses empowers us to rely on Him.

And even when we have to step out in faith, when God's presence feels minimal, God is peace. "And the peace of God, which transcends all understanding, will guard your hearts and your minds in Christ Jesus" (Philippians 4:7). As we allow Him to fill the spaces in our spirit, His peace satisfies and protects our souls. God wants to do more in our lives than we can even imagine. In the midst of distractions, we can open up our spirit for Him to work. His Holy Spirit working in us is an all-consuming supernatural gift that does not rely on circumstances. Awareness of His Spirit provides the connection to His peace.

It can be easy, in our busy lives, to try to grasp God's peace on the run. We cannot find His peace without taking the time to focus on Jesus and the gift He has provided while abiding in His presence. I have to remind myself, when life gets busy, to focus on God's peace. My heart and mind get uneasy during these times, and my focus becomes self-centered. Once again I lose connection with God because I have placed my life ahead of His presence. I lose peace and have to reconnect immediately.

Our thoughts race to places of failing God. It feels like He has a microscope on our lives. Viewing God as someone who always critiques our every action relinquishes the peace He gives as a gift. His ways are perfect (Psalm 18:30). He is so much more than the flawed human version we project on Him. We are not failures in His eyes.

Taking our thoughts captive and redirecting them to God's love deepens our peace. Jesus' death on the Cross covers our sins in the past, present, and future. He loves us because we are His children, not because we perform well. His peace rests on us.

God is a God of action. He is always at work. He has even worked in my life in ways I haven't even known to ask for. We may not know what life holds for us in this moment, but we don't have to, He does. God is already at work.

*"For I know the plans I have for you," declares the LORD, "plans to prosper you and not to harm you, plans to give you hope and a future."*
*—Jeremiah 29:11*

Jeremiah 29:11 is my favorite passage of Scripture. It reminds me that God knows the plans for my life. He desires for me to prosper and not be hurt. He is my protector. My hope is in Him. He is in my future. God is already there. He knows the outcome. My soul has peace in those words. My God is an amazing God of action.

When we don't experience confidence, we feel heavy-spirited and sad-hearted. But we can worship God because of who He is, not because of who we are or how we feel. Jesus is at the top of our priority list. Joy is a product of our worship. Our bodies may not feel like worshipping and placing Him first. We may be burdened by our experiences or the spiritual warfare waging within us. However, our hearts need to be engaged. Focus on God and allow Him to create a desire within you to see the work He is performing in you.

We have to submit to the work He wants and has planned for us. Rejoicing in the Lord's perfect plan can happen even when the craziness and busyness of the world swirl around us. At that moment, we can find Jesus near us satisfying our souls and soothing our spirits. "Where can I go from your Spirit? Where can I flee from your presence?" (Psalm 139:7). He is always working.

God is our strength. Where can you be bold and stand before God in the midst of all that is going on in your life? God is our shelter and strength, always ready to help in times of trouble.

*So we will not be afraid, even if the earth is shaken and mountains fall into the ocean depths; even if the seas roar and rage, and the hills are shaken by the violence.*

*—Psalm 46:2–3 GNT*

Through this adventure of becoming more aware of God, my trust in Him has increased. When I needed support, He helped me through.

His Spirit helped me when I became weak in spirit. When I reached out to God, His Spirit filled me with His strength. I became more aware of His power and needed to rely on mine less.

We do not have to do it all. God is there as our strength to propel us to the work He desires to do in and through us according to His power that is at work in us. The same power that was at work in raising Jesus from the dead is the same power that is available to us (Acts 1:8), a power that cannot be conjured up within but only through our spiritual connection to Christ. God's strength is stronger than anything we could ever imagine, and it is freely given to us. Connecting to His power source provides us an insurmountable existence, revealing His glory through our lives.

God is with us. Continue to seek Him in all things throughout the day. Is there a time today when you can release the distractions and listen to the Lord? Are there things you can put off until later to be able to be more aware of Him in your Spirit? Can you stand boldly with arms wide open to receive Him?

Our spiritual connection comes from seeking Him in all circumstances. To pursue God, we must first begin to build trust in who He is and what He does. Submitting to His power in our lives and giving up our abilities by submitting to Him empowers us in trust and love.

*Submission* is a hard word for me. My experiences in life have taught me that if you submit to someone it gives them the ability to abuse the situation. Having been taken advantage of in these experiences taught me to put on a tough façade and not let anyone see vulnerability. Those experiences were hurtful and caused a lot of baggage in my life. It has taken a long time to embrace the freedom, safety, and protection in submitting to Christ. Others may take advantage of you, but Christ never will.

Humbling ourselves to the almighty power God has and the love He grants is freeing. Knowing God has our back in all situations also gives us the ability to step out in faith. Submission is a move to a deeper connection and spiritual growth. God doesn't require us to submit because He is a cruel, oppressive ruler. Rather, humbly submitting and surrendering daily to a loving God who wants us to be the best we can be brings peace and blessings. Trusting Him builds a hopeful heart and a peaceful presence.

Being aware of God's presence isn't a truth I learned quickly. After giving my life to the Lord in high school, I chose to walk away from the church. The baggage of life weighed heavily on me. My thoughts were negative and chaotic. I had no hope for a bright future. Being worthy of any love was far from any dream I could imagine.

Then, I met Dave Jauss, a nice guy who said he wanted to spend his life with me. I wanted to do life with him too. We married and had babies. But I dragged my baggage into our relationship. I was acutely aware of all my faults and my controlling behavior; I no longer had a connection with God. More and more mistakes were made and embraced. More and more distance separated me from God's presence.

At the breaking point of my marriage, I felt empty, hopeless, and alone. A counselor asked me when I had experienced the most peace in my life. Immediately I knew. It was when I was going to church and felt the incredible presence of Jesus in my life. That day, I made a plan to go back to church and seek the God I once knew. The God who loves me enough to give His Son for my sins, even the ones I had not made yet. The one who had never left me even though I built walls and pushed Him away. The Jesus who had a plan for my life, not the one I thought was going to strike me down with every move I made. The one who saved my marriage from the brink of destruction.

Going to church doesn't stop our negative thoughts or our bad behavior. It doesn't increase our awareness of God on its own. Be engaged. Be aware. Be with Him. Be conscious of the Holy Spirit's existence within us. Be still while in the forward motion of a busy life. Just be.

Being in His presence is an act of obedience. Obedience is not automatic. It grows hand-in-hand with our trusting God and who He is. Our obedience proves our love for God. Acting in obedience is proof of what we believe. And God is glorified through our obedience. Increasing awareness of the Holy Spirit increases our desire to be obedient. Decreasing our thought of power depending on us and growing the Spirit's power within us releases the damper that holds us back from glorifying Him.

In Acts 6, the 12 apostles were overstretched with the needs of the expanding church. Responsibilities included not only the spiritual ministry of preaching the Word of God and prayer, but also a material ministry of service to their community. The church was mostly made up of Jews separated into different cultural groups. The Greek-speaking believers felt they were being discriminated against in the daily food lines. The apostles needed more leaders to help calm the groups. They came together and chose seven trustworthy men.

When the Spirit of God is alive inside us, it changes everything. Spirit-filled people live into the purposes of God. We understand we have embraced our place in the story of God.

We live the story of a victim when we get stuck in a spirit of helplessness, fear, or negativity. Living a life filled with the Holy Spirit changes and grows a life of victory. A life of victory creates boldness.

In order to accommodate the growing church and its needs, Stephen was one of the men chosen. He was a dynamic leader, full of God's grace. He was a man full of faith and the Holy Spirit (vv. 1–7). Miracles were happening, and his knowledge far exceeded the men of the synagogue. In secret, these men hired false witnesses to stir up the anger toward Stephen. His circumstances became unbearable, yet he stood with boldness. He was taken into custody and forced to stand before the High Council. The witnesses lied and projected negativity toward Stephen. He had a choice—fall to the negativity and the circumstance or stand boldly, allowing the Holy Spirit to work through Him. "All who were sitting in the Sanhedrin looked intently at Stephen, and they saw that his face was like the face of an angel" (Acts 6:15).

Stephen chose to reveal the work of God's Spirit in him (Acts 7). He recounted the Old Testament history and ended with a rebuke for the Sanhedrin's murder of Jesus. When he finished, Stephen looked up to heaven and saw the glory of God and Jesus at the right hand of God (v. 56). Furious with this declaration, the members of the Sanhedrin stoned Stephen. Living in an intimate relationship with the Holy Spirit, Stephen died as Jesus had. He was the first Christian martyr. He had no resentment toward his murderers. "Then he fell on his knees and cried out, 'Lord, do not hold this sin against them.' When he had said this, he fell asleep" (v. 60).

The story of Stephen was not one without struggle. But it was a story of a victor, not a victim. He embraced the Holy Spirit and was aware of God's Spirit within him. The enemy wants us to go down a victim path, falling into the darkness he desires us to live in, far away from God's Spirit. When we are aware of His Spirit and embrace the amazing power God offers us, others see the glory of God in us. Stephen forgave the men who stoned him and asked God to forgive them. He didn't seek revenge or allow his anger to rage. His face looked like the face of an angel. Something transcendent had happened in his submission, obedience, and reliance on God. Stephen embraced the power and strength of God. He knew God sits on the throne.

As our faith grows, our knowledge of God's Word expands, our awareness of the Holy Spirit thrives, and God's work within us flourishes. We will always have experiences that distract and upset us. Be bold and stand before God with open arms ready to receive His work in and through us. God is with us through it all.

We have distractions and heartaches in this roller coaster of life. The peace that has come from knowing God can do anything "according to his power" is overwhelming. "And the peace of God, which transcends all understanding, will guard your hearts and your minds in Christ Jesus" (Philippians 4:7).

Stand boldly aware of a great God who is always at work in us. God desires us to remain before Him and ask openly. Don't underestimate the power of His work in and through us! If we find no conflict in our lives, then we are avoiding an opportunity to be courageous. Shaking off the hindrances that hold us back from awareness of the mighty power of God at work within us creates boldness.

*By this we shall know that we are of the truth, and reassure our hearts before him whenever our hearts condemn us; for God is greater than our hearts, and he knows everything. Beloved, if our hearts do not condemn us, we have confidence before God.*

*—1 John 3:19–21 RSV*

Boldness is a virtue we should aspire to in seeking to glorify the Lord. God is not a weak God. We are not weak believers when we are aware of His Spirit with us.

Going to church and immersing ourselves in learning who God is and who we are with Him creates a new awareness. Life changes. Our lives begin to move in a new direction of glorifying God. We need to listen to God more and to ourselves less. The awareness of His power at work within us takes us into a closer connection with God.

As we continue this spiritual travel, allowing God to work in us, we will be more aware of His presence. Together we are bold before God as the chaotic world swirls around us. Our complicated lives can be a distraction, but our connection to His presence increases as we rinse our spirits of the busyness that flusters us.

Awareness of God's Holy Spirit within us uncovers an understanding of His will for our lives as we move deeper into the work He is doing in us.

# Understanding His Will

## CHAPTER FIVE

Possessing knowledge is important, but a spiritual connection with Christ leads to an empathetic soulful recognition, and recognizing the presence of God grants a deeper understanding of what He desires. I realized I was standing in God's way with my busy life and to-do lists. I couldn't see His desires because my wishes were drowning my spirit. Much like the distractions I placed in the depths of my soul, my busy life blocked the deeper connection and understanding I needed to propel myself into glorifying God according to His power.

I began to focus on God's desires for me—the connection of my soul with His. I had been focusing on the to-dos that portrayed me as a dutiful Christian woman who was leading her children in dutiful Christian ways. This journey was revealing my selfish intent. I was trying to fit a mold of what people expected of a Christian, not what God expected of me.

I had to uncover the contrary ideas that inhibited my understanding of God's will in my life. Negative ideas planted in our innermost thoughts come from different experiences. The unfavorable words Christians say to Christians builds a wall of misunderstanding of what is important—His will or others' words.

At church one Sunday, I shared my love for speaking with a dearly respected woman in our church. I told her about an event where I spoke to a group of women in baseball. I also shared I was writing devotions for the Baseball Chapel website. I talked about the great feedback I received regarding my speaking and writing. I asked her to pray for me as I thought deeper about pursuing more engagements and opportunities.

I was stunned at her response. With a chuckle, she responded, "God needs meek and mild women to represent Him, and you are not one of those." Were her hurtful words spoken with laughter supposed to make the blow easier? It didn't. I thought God was calling me to speak and write. My heart and her words did not match. And it was her words that replayed in my mind when I should have sought God for understanding. Out of fear, I reverted to old tendencies and shut down.

This experience played in my mind as I sought a deeper understanding of God's desires. I realized that believing others' words derail our forward motion to glorify God. These are the circumstances that deter us from God's will, redirecting us to the will of others. I continued to write and speak after the incident but sought out no further opportunities. I saw other respected Christian speakers who were outgoing and louder than I, but I continued to hear the negative words of the woman from my church.

We allow others' comments to make us strive to please people, question our worth, and question what God is calling us to do. The negative comment from the lady at church hindered my momentum in pursuing what God desired. The hindrance of moving forward lasted for ten years. Ten years of negative thinking and devaluing myself as a person who could be used by God, all because one woman made a rude comment.

But sometimes even people's well-intentioned words hurt us. Like when tragedy strikes and we're told, "It is the will of God." When a child is abused, when tragedy beyond comprehension inserts itself into our lives, is it the will of God? As we look at the biblical understanding of the will of God and who God is, we do not see a God who approves of abuse. He calls us to love one another.

Over the time of making room for the Holy Spirit, I began to see me as God sees me. I am a child of God created in His image. He created every aspect of my personality for His purpose. And whether I perceive these issues as negative, or even if others criticize me, He knew at my formation that these are characteristics that make me who He wants me to be. Standing in God's way inhibits the fullness He can accomplish according to His power. The enemy can use our thoughts to take us in a direction that is contrary to God's plan.

I am not a mold. I am different—not what most dutiful church ladies may see as the perfect Christian woman. Yes, I am bold. I am loud. I am fun. I am who God made me to be. My journey sent me on a quest to understand who He wants me to be according to Him. Was there more He wanted to do, things I never considered? What is His will for me?

Understanding the will of God has long perplexed me. How are we to know the will of God? Am I doing the will of God? Is the will of God what's best for me? Do I want to do the will of God, or do I want to do what I want to do?

I want to believe life is in my control. I can bulldoze through and accomplish what needs to be done. My lists grow. My lack of success in managing them multiplies. Pushing our will on God this way breeds discouragement. But understanding His will induces power beyond understanding.

*Do not conform to the pattern of this world, but be transformed by the renewing of your mind. Then you will be able to test and approve what God's will is—his good, pleasing and perfect will.*
*—Romans 12:2*

Transformed lives lead to renewal and understanding. When our minds are renewed as children of God, we can test and understand the good, pleasing, and perfect will of God. With a renewed connection with Jesus, I began to wait for Him.

Life doesn't always allow us to find a cozy corner with a cup of tea, our Bible, and complete silence. If your life is like mine, especially when my boys were young, there are crashes and screams, cries and needs, dogs barking, doors slamming, and many other bumps in the night breaking the quietness of our homes. I have experienced His presence deep in my soul even in those chaotic times. Being more aware of God's Spirit within us connects us to Him even in the busyness.

Chaos continues to swirl, but God is with us. Understanding God's will initially requires us to see our need for Christ. He works for the good of those who love Him, for those who have been called (Romans 8:28–29). Each day we should continue to be more like Christ. Conforming to His image, understanding His will.

In Matthew 5, the Beatitudes begin, "Blessed are the poor in spirit, for theirs is the kingdom of heaven" (v. 3). To be poor in spirit means being defeated and broken. Our need for Christ begins when we recognize our poorness of spirit. When we are at the end of the rope of fulfilling our own desires, God is most ready to fill us with more of Him. Jesus wants to connect with all people. We can reach out to God when we recognize our need for Him.

As I increased my awareness of God's presence, my yearning for more of Him also increased. My spirit had been depleted in the midst of my busy life. The closer I drew to Him, the more room I made, the more desire grew in my heart to be in His presence, wanting to understand His will. Pleasing God became a stronger desire.

Stepping out in faith to understand His will takes extreme trust and awareness of His Spirit within us. We surrender our will to God, humble ourselves, and submit to Him. Knowing Jesus as a living entity, with whom we have a relationship, draws us closer to His Spirit. We learn to love and serve Him with our whole hearts, deep in our souls.

I discovered I lack knowledge of God's will because of my disdain for submitting. I don't hate submission to God, but I struggle with the overall concept of submission. I believed when you submit you are kicked around, taken advantage of, seen as weak, and walked over. Confusing submission with oppression was the world I lived in for many years. In my mind, submission led to bullying, abusing, and overpowering another. Strength won, humbleness died. I built walls around my soul. I wouldn't let God in. I didn't allow myself to be vulnerable to His love and kindness. I didn't want to be taken advantage of by others or by Him.

Submission is an offering to God, a sacrifice to Him. It is not to be confused with oppression. Godly submission is being a loving member of God's family. Submission is not as much an action as an attitude, an attitude of God leading us into a righteous relationship.

*Submit yourselves, then, to God. Resist the devil, and he will flee from you. Come near to God and he will come near to you. Wash your hands, you sinners, and purify your hearts, you double-minded. Grieve, mourn and wail. Change your laughter to mourning and your joy to gloom. Humble yourselves before the Lord, and he will lift you up.*

*—James 4:7–10*

Pride hinders submission. The more I submit, the more clearly I see the selfish spirit I carried around when I relied on my power, not His. When did the "I" disease invade my soul? What have I done to lose my belief that Jesus is King? How did I forget He takes care of me and my circumstances? Who is bigger than God? How have I taken God's ability into my hands?

Rooting out the sinful attitude of pride opens the doors of our hearts to God's desire. Submission allows the Holy Spirit to work in us and enables us to glorify God. Once we are rid of defiant attitudes and allow the authority of Christ to lead us, the Holy Spirit can begin to move in us and open our understanding of His desires.

When my boys were little, they loved to tell me that I wanted them to be perfect. This statement came after their bad behavior landed them in time-out. I would quickly remind them we would never be perfect. However, God desires for us to become more like Christ. When we have power washed our spirits to allow the Holy Spirit to move freely in us, Jesus has room to move in our souls. We begin to look more like Christ through our actions and our reactions as we seek to be mindful of God and His desires.

> *Dear friends, now we are children of God, and what we will be has not yet been made known. But we know that when Christ appears, we shall be like him, for we shall see him as he is.*
>
> *—1 John 3:2*

Being like Christ is a slow process and will not be fully achieved until we are face-to-face with our Savior. God desires for us to be more like Christ and glorify Him in what we say, do, and are. Each of the steps we take in seeking the abundant life God desires for us brings us closer to His likeness and understanding of His will—both the revealed will written in the Bible and His unrevealed will, which He may unveil over time.

The revealed will of God, found in Scripture, guides us in knowledge. "Rejoice always, pray continually, give thanks in all circumstances; for this is God's will for you in Christ Jesus" (1 Thessalonians 5:16–18). To rejoice always means to have an attitude of joy at all times. We cannot be cheerful at all times. There will always be times of sorrow and grief on this earth. But just as Paul learned the "secret of being content in any and every situation" (Philippians 4:12), we too can experience the strength to get through our circumstances and slowly achieve a type of joy or contentment in trusting that God's desires for us are good. We can focus on His goodness even as we compare it to how vile the world and our circumstances are. He wants to give us hope so we can have an attitude of joy, even in the chaos.

Rejoicing always doesn't mean we will never be sad or have feelings of despair. It means we make a choice to rejoice in respect to who Christ is and what He has done for us. As Christians, we are living in a world that does not belong to us, and that means life will be difficult. We will feel sadness and despair. We don't have to dismiss those feelings.

Jesus both wept and experienced joy when faced with the suffering He would experience on the Cross. Trials and suffering are not joyful in the moment, but in submitting to Christ's desires and ways, we are blessed by His righteousness and love. Rejoicing is God's will for us.

In the weeks before Christmas one year, my stepfather was diagnosed with metastatic cancer. This seemingly healthy man passed two weeks after diagnosis. The same week he died, a dear friend was driving behind her son when his motorcycle hit sand on the road and caused him to crash. He died instantly. These circumstances can bring the end of natural joy very quickly. Christmas was not the same for either of our families.

The reasons we are happy on a day-to-day basis can be taken from us without warning—jobs, family, money, homes, friends. I saw this firsthand during the following weeks. I got home from my stepfather's funeral only to attend the wake for my friend's son. As I approached her, she was visibly weak and broken. My heart broke even more than I thought it could. "Pray for me," she begged as we embraced. "Always," I promised.

Her world had changed. But her God was the same. She knew it and begged for support. I prayed. Every day I prayed. When the Lord put it on my heart, I would send her a text to remind her of my prayers and love. A few months later when we had time alone to talk and listen, she said, "I felt the prayers. God is good." She smiled through the pain, allowing God's joy to replace the fear of her current condition and what was to come.

 *And they offered great sacrifices that day and rejoiced, for God had made them rejoice with great joy; the women and children also rejoiced. And the joy of Jerusalem was heard far away.*
*—Nehemiah 12:43 ESV*

God produces joy in His people. When we place our trust in a relationship with Christ, God produces and gives us joy. The joy God provides is a spiritual joy, not dependent on one experience or the next. Looking for something or someone to give us joy constructs a cycle of highs and lows. A sequence of, "I will be happy and joyful when."

In *Choose Joy: Because Happiness Isn't Enough*, Kay Warren writes, "Joy is the settled assurance that God is in control of all the details of my life, the quiet confidence that ultimately everything is going to be all right, and the determined choice to praise God in all things." The determined choice of trusting God leads to spiritual joy from the Holy Spirit. Rejoice always.

God's will for us is to pray continually. The boys and I were driving on a busy highway heading to another baseball town when traffic came to a screeching halt. Soon after, as we crept along, two ambulances and a fire truck flew by in the emergency lane. "Let's pray for the people in the accident," one of the boys requested. I began to pray out loud. Another son screamed, "Mom you can't pray; you are driving!" How many times do we postpone prayer because of the chaos around us—kids, driving, disorder, chaos, or tragedy? We don't have to wait for the right time or perfect place. We need to pray continually and maintain an ongoing conversation with God.

Stop your running thoughts and actions. Prayer is a conversation with the dearest friend you could ever have. Be you. Talk to Him as you would talk to anyone else. Acknowledge His presence.

Be vulnerable. Ask Him to teach you how to pray, to give you a heart and desire for prayer. He is listening. Let His Spirit wash over your soul as you pray to the Almighty God. He will give you what you need.

When my kids were little, my husband traveled for 10–14 days at a time. At that point in life, happiness came in the form of being able to use the bathroom alone. It rarely happened. When I woke up in the mornings I was already tired. The days gave no rest. I hoped I could get through the day. I had made it through the day before but still wasn't convinced.

Many days our only goal is to survive. We will. Having a direct line open to Jesus makes us feel more alive. Even if you only have a small whisper left in you, keep praying.

God's revealed will of "give thanks in all circumstances" is difficult when life is hard. But it becomes easier the more we acknowledge and understand that God is in control. A thankful heart can change our attitude and draw us closer to Christ and others. We can learn from the Apostle Paul. He lived through great adversity, yet continued to be thankful.

*Speaking to one another with psalms, hymns, and songs from the Spirit. Sing and make music from your heart to the Lord, always giving thanks to God the Father for everything, in the name of our Lord Jesus Christ.*

*—Ephesians 5:19–20*

Paul gave thanks, but not because of what was going on around him. Being imprisoned made for harsh circumstances. He gave thanks because of who God is. Appreciating Jesus and what He did deepens our relationship and exposes the blessings.

The month of November brings about a flood of posts on social media announcing what people are thankful for in their lives. I admit I am one of these people. The month is a time to focus on the gratefulness we feel all year. It reminds us of the need to be thankful each moment. It began for me years ago when I heard about a woman who kept a gratitude journal. She used it to refocus her mind from worry and anxiety to positive thoughts and thankfulness.

My thoughts were negative, my hope drained. But what did I have to lose? I began a gratitude journal.

I opened my new journal, turning the crisp page to the first fully lined one. I began to write but stopped after *"I am thankful for."* I waited for something to come to mind. Nothing. I couldn't think of one thing I was grateful for in my life. I could quickly list the "poor me" items floating around my brain. I thought of things others are thankful for in their lives.

Was I thankful I was alive? Yes, but I had no joy or purpose. Was I thankful for the roof over my head? At the time I would have been happier living in a box on a beach instead of where I lived. What about having food in the fridge? Honestly, I'd rather be eating out. These thoughts startled me.

*Was I really this ungrateful?*

Yes. More than I ever dreamed I could be.

My husband's friend asked him if I was always as happy as I appeared. He responded yes, but not even he knows what negative thoughts I can have. Being viewed as a happy person doesn't always mean the thoughts rattling around inside my head were happy. Worry, anxiety, failure, lack of self-worth, and ungratefulness often swirled from one thought to another despite the smile I was wearing.

The journaling exercise revealed something about myself, and I used it to form new patterns. The first entry came: *I am thankful for the earth.* The next day: *I am thankful for the sky.* Then, the sun, a bird flying by, the laughter of my kids. A few weeks in, I wrote, *I am thankful for life.* My heart changed along with my thoughts. I looked for positive occurrences throughout the day to write in my journal. My heart softened. My focus changed.

## BEING THANKFUL . . .

made me realize my life was better than I thought, better than my attitude deserved. Gratitude doesn't come naturally to some. However, I forced myself to focus on the things around me. With a discerning eye, I began to see the value of my surroundings differently.

## BEING THANKFUL . . .

helped me see the beauty in the world. When you are looking for things to be thankful for you will find them. They may have always been there, you just may not have seen them. Even in the mirror. "I praise you because I am fearfully and wonderfully made; your works are wonderful, I know that full well" (Psalm 139:14).

## BEING THANKFUL . . .

increased my faith. "Therefore I tell you, do not worry about your life, what you will eat or drink; or about your body, what you will wear. Is not life more than food, and the body more than clothes? Look at the birds of the air; they do not sow or reap or store away in barns, and yet your heavenly Father feeds them. Are you not much more valuable than they?" (Matthew 6:25–26).

## BEING THANKFUL . . .

gave me hope. Being thankful changes our perspective of God's gifts in our lives, and it helps create within us a giving and more humble spirit. "Be completely humble and gentle; be patient, bearing with one another in love" (Ephesians 4:2). A grateful heart changes our attitude and our view.

Understanding God's will to rejoice always, pray continually, and give thanks in all circumstances comes naturally when good things happen. It's not so easy when things are busy and problems arise. But even in the midst of our busy lives, when things are not going as planned, we can fulfill His will when growing in our spiritual lives. As I walked this journey with the Lord, I found understanding God's will was directly linked to my connection to the Holy Spirit. The closer I drew to Him, the more freely I could rejoice, pray, and be thankful. I began looking for opportunities to allow the Holy Spirit to work. Obeying the will of God continually prepares us for all God desires to do in us.

Another aspect of God's revealed will is to be sanctified (1 Thessalonians 4:3). God sanctifies us through the process of His forgiveness of our sins and by conforming us to the image of His Son. When we give our lives to Christ, our lives are new, and the old is gone. Christ's perfection is placed on us.

I once overheard a preteen say, "I've said that prayer a hundred times, and then I make bad decisions again." He was speaking about the sinner's prayer. I felt as though this young man were talking to me. I too have walked into church burdened and full of guilt for something I have done. I too try to renew my forgiveness by reciting old prayers. We don't have to renew our forgiveness. It has been given freely. We try to pay God back with our guilt and condemnation of self when Jesus has already covered us with His righteousness. We need to confess our sins to Him, receive His forgiveness, and move forward with a goal of being more like Christ.

We are sanctified and Christlike, yet we still sin. As we grow closer to Christ and strengthen our connection with Him, each day we will act more and more like Christ. Sanctification is work initiated by Christ, not a single act but a progressive, ongoing process. The process begins when we receive Christ as our Savior and is not finished until we are face-to-face with Jesus. Let's say it together: "We are a work in progress."

The revealed will of God is also to do good in His name. "For it is God's will that by doing good you should silence the ignorant talk of foolish people" (1 Peter 2:15). Here Peter is talking to the church about submitting to authority, whether they are Christian believers in power or not. He tells them it is necessary to fulfill the will of God in the world. Being good citizens silences the ignorant, who think you are a danger to society. Doing good is not the same as the list of what we think makes us look like a good Christian. It is the acts we commit in response to lives renewed by Christ. And people will take notice— not only those who don't believe but also those who sit beside you in Bible study and church.

I can easily fall into the "do good" trap. I believe the more Christian I act, the better mom and wife I'll be. But the "do good" trap only binds the time and energy I need to leave open for connecting with the Lord.

Why can't I just get it already? Why can't I be the somber, quiet Christian woman who sits in a beautifully decorated corner with a cup of tea, a warm blanket, and my Bible, enjoying her intimate time with God? But we can't spend all our time sitting in corners spending time with God; at some point we have to get up and share His love with others.

Since my family spends so much of our time on the go, I spend time with God in some of the most unlikely places. I spend hours traveling in the car, sitting in airports, walking through baseball stadiums, meandering through streets in a city, chasing after my husband and boys. I call my life organized chaos . . . mostly organized but with a lot of chaos.

We don't always live the "do good" life in our crazy busy lives. We get frustrated, ignore others, and treat others badly. Our outward actions give others foolish things to claim about Christians. We don't always get it right, but a deeper connection with Christ allows us to return to the good that results from glorifying Him. When we live a Christlike life, we discover an understanding of His will. Rejoice. Pray. Give thanks. We are sanctified and called to do good.

In understanding God's revealed will, we are positioned to better hear His unrevealed will. His unrevealed will contains the secrets He holds closely. God has not revealed all He knows. Some secrets belong only to Him. "The secret things belong to the LORD our God, but the things revealed belong to us and to our children forever, that we may follow all the words of this law" (Deuteronomy 29:29). Moving out of His way and allowing Him to be God is all in preparation for the generous future He has for us.

The unrevealed will of God is hard to see during the duration of a trial or a blessing. We see more clearly when the season of time has passed. As I learned to make room for God, trust and obedience were essential for change. I had to trust the Lord. In submitting to and obeying the revealed will of God, His unrevealed will can be understood in a more profound way.

Our family was blessed when my husband and I became foster parents to three amazing babies. Not all at the same time. (Thank God!) Certified on a Friday, a baby was placed in our home less than 48 hours later—the day after Christmas. She, as well the following two foster children in our home, had been born addicted to heroin. Her mother left her at the hospital as she had others before. Being a foster parent took lots of patience and love, not for the baby, but the system. I struggled with the fact that my husband and I had no control, no say, and no ability to change any of the fostering processes.

We believed we were making a difference in the life of the baby. What we didn't see through all the frustration, trials, and struggles were the blessings we were receiving along the way. It was only after the long days and nights of being obedient while loving and protecting the baby in our house that we could see His will. Even without our understanding at the time, God's will triumphed in each of their lives. The outcomes were more impactful than anything we could have ever prayed for the children. We rejoiced. We prayed. We gave thanks in all circumstances. He worked His desires.

The goal of understanding God's will is not ferreting out the secrets of God but comprehending, obeying, and moving forward in the revealed will of God. As our relationship strengthens, our trust and obedience will follow. A renewed mind and a transformed life lead to mature discernment. The Bible does not reveal to us where we should live, what we should major in during college, what job to accept, or which person to marry. The answers to those decisions come from discernment based on biblical truth and spiritual connection.

I wrote this book because of a journey I took after my pastor asked a question. The question nagged me, returning to my thoughts often. As I delved into the process of understanding God's will, I wrote and rewrote the Scripture that pointed to God's revealed will in my life. As I sat to write this chapter, I began with prayer. I have a self-made prayer book I use to guide my prayers each day. On that day it read: *Pray for spiritual boldness in what I say, do, and write. Confidence. Courage. Conviction.*

With confidence in who God is, I rejoice. Conversing in prayer with my Lord and Savior, my courage swells. Being grateful for the blessings God pours on me, my conviction to be more Christlike thrives. I don't sit down knowing what I will write. I often struggle with the words I think I should place on the page. I write the first word, then another, rejoicing, praying, and giving thanks.

We don't know what may come next in our busy lives. Relying on and obeying the revealed will of God propels us to a place of trusting our next steps to the secrets He holds close to His heart. "On the day I called, You answered me; You made me bold with strength in my soul" (Psalm 138:3 NASB).

Jesus' life, ministry, and teachings provide us with significant influence on the importance of realizing God's will. He lived a life that perfectly demonstrated conformity to God's will. It proved to the disciples and others that His life did not take a natural course.

Before His Crucifixion, Jesus and the disciples went to Gethsemane. Once there, Jesus went off to be alone. "Going a little farther, he fell with his face to the ground and prayed, 'My Father, if it is possible, may this cup be taken from me. Yet not as I will, but as you will'" (Matthew 26:39). Jesus acknowledged His desire but submitted to the Father's will. Aware His death was imminent, Jesus didn't want to suffer but wanted to fulfill the will of God—for our sake.

Not only was Jesus to do the will of God, but His disciples did also. He taught His disciples to pray.

*This, then, is how you should pray: "Our Father in heaven, hallowed be your name, your kingdom come, your will be done, on earth as it is in heaven. Give us today our daily bread. And forgive us our debts, as we also have forgiven our debtors. And lead us not into temptation, but deliver us from the evil one."*

*—Matthew 6:9–13*

Jesus' prayer teaches us to long for God's will. Being a child of God we are not called to do according to our standards but to His.

To learn and understand God's revealed will is to be able to live out the divine. It occurs through our appropriate behavior. Our inability to obey continues to exist alongside God's divine sovereignty. God has to direct us to perceive His will. Then He enables us to fulfill His desires.

*Now may the God of peace, who through the blood of the eternal covenant brought back from the dead our Lord Jesus, that great Shepherd of the sheep, equip you with everything good for doing his will, and may he work in us what is pleasing to him, through Jesus Christ, to whom be glory for ever and ever. Amen.*

*—Hebrews 13:20–21*

As we fulfill God's revealed will, He renews our thoughts, attitudes, and actions. They become a natural spillover from what's inside. Not just knowing but applying His will to how we live each and every day draws us into a deeper relationship, strengthening and emboldening us. Allowing the Holy Spirit to penetrate our soul creates an atmosphere of submitting to God's desire, and understanding His will pulls us ever closer to what God wants to do in and through us.

# Listening for Guidance

## CHAPTER SIX

Let's say it together again: "We are a work in progress." I know I am. The work God is doing in me doesn't just magically happen. Salvation didn't turn me into a perfect Christian. The work in me is a process of my relationship with Him, becoming more like Christ, being more aware of the Holy Spirit living in me, and understanding His will for me.

As I delved deeper and purposefully searched to know and understand God's desires, I saw my tendencies to fall into the "do good" life over and over. And of course the "do good" life relied on my own abilities, not His. I rely on my energy and resources to figure life out. I was allowing my busy life to take the place of Jesus and inhibit the work He wanted to accomplish. I continued to evaluate my heart on a consistent basis and identify the distractions that took over my moments of peace. Spiritual attacks continued to come and go as I relied on the power of Christ and His Holy Spirit to infiltrate the deep crevices of my soul. I fell to fear and anxiety, busyness, and filling my life with rubbish.

Where I grew up in the South, I was often surrounded by Christians. Somehow, though, I didn't learn how to interact with the Holy Spirit on my own. There were many strong believers around town who seemed to interact with Him in a way I was unfamiliar with. "Listen for God. He will tell you what you need to hear." "God said to me . . ." "Sweet Jesus, speak to me." "Girl, God is talking. Just perk up those ears."

Young girls can be freaked out a little by talk like that when they are not accustomed to it. I was one who was freaked out.

Were these people crazy? I didn't want to go away to Dorothea Dix, our state mental hospital. "Dix Hill" was not a place anyone wanted to go. I continued to question, "Can God speak to me? Can we hear Him?" I knew if He had answers, I wanted them.

Listening for God's guidance is not crazy. He does speak. In the beginning, God spoke, and light, sky, water, land, sun, moon, creatures, plants, and man came to be. His words were powerful then and are powerful now. My soul longed for the words of guidance Jesus desired for me. I yearned to be guided by His voice.

When I was in elementary school, I was often in trouble. I am a talker. My teacher disciplined me for engaging my fellow students in conversation at inappropriate times. If my classmates didn't want to talk, it was OK—I talked anyway. The woman at my church wasn't wrong when she said I am not meek and mild.

I talk to anyone and in any situation. God made me this way. Sometimes the gifts God gives us can also be a hindrance. The ability to talk is good when you are a speaker, a counselor, or when in large crowds. The drawback is when we talk but never listen. Listening is a gift and strength for many, but it is one I am not naturally gifted at. I have to work on my listening skills all the time. My teacher told me in elementary school to zip my lips and throw away the key, and my husband now tells me the same thing by not saying much. I am a slow learner. Busyness combined with an anxious spirit makes it easier to speak than listen.

When being busy and anxious leads to talking instead of listening, it stops us from hearing others and God. Listening for God's voice is not the same as listening to others. His spirit speaks into our souls. Our overthinking and hurried lives clog our spirit and inhibit our listening for God's leading.

When some people accept Christ as their Savior, they immediately begin to hear God speak. Not so for everyone. We have to learn to listen. Various obstacles prevent us from hearing God. Maybe we feel unworthy to hear God's voice. Or maybe we feel our sin is too awful to be forgiven completely. Surely our past is too bad to allow us to hear God speak. We just aren't good enough. *Stop!* These are lies. When we become a child of God, we are worthy of all the blessings God wants to pour over us. Hearing His guidance is a gift and a blessing. Take each negative thought captive. Believe He longs to speak to you.

Being fearful of what God might say also inhibits our ability to hear. It was such an honor to listen to a missionary family's story of how they heard from God. He told them to pack up everything they owned and go to Africa to serve. Sitting in church with three little boys and a husband who traveled for weeks and months, I was terrified to ask God what he wanted me to do. I wasn't able to do what they did—go to Africa—even though I had long desired to go. I couldn't take three little boys to a foreign country and serve when my husband's job would not permit him to go with us. I am not asking God what He wants. What if He answers?

These were my actual thoughts. I did not want to hear God tell me to do something I couldn't or didn't want to do. See, if I didn't ask, He wouldn't tell, and then I didn't have to be disobedient. And I didn't want to be disobedient. (Like I said, I'm a slow learner.) Disobedience started with the phrase *I am not.* Fear stops us from approaching God for His guidance. Understanding His will for us to rejoice, pray, and give thanks (1 Thessalonians 5:16–18) gives us the confidence to approach Him, knowing He will work for the good of those who love Him. Being afraid of what God might say stops us from being more like Jesus and doing the good He has called us to do.

Our prayers can also get in the way of hearing from God. Prayer can be a pleading and begging session of one-way talk: *God, give me money. God, give me an answer. God, give me a job. God, give me a life. I need to hear from You. I beg You.* But it's about God's will, not ours. It's about having more of Him and less of ourselves.

I have found myself begging God to reveal Himself to me. *Do it already! I don't have time to wait. I have things to do. People to talk to.* I'm not always that pushy with Him, but aren't there times in our lives when we are just too busy to allow God to work in us? Giving Him a list of what we think we need or want is easier than allowing Him to do His work in His time.

I know God has a sense of humor, and I think He must laugh at me a lot. When I push my desires or plans on Him, He laughs. Oh, sweet Jesus chuckles. I can hear Him saying it now, "Oh, that girl." God's plans are much better than ours.

When our emotional pipes get clogged with fear, busyness, or our desires, our spirits are not able to connect with Jesus. "Whether you turn to the right or to the left, your ears will hear a voice behind you, saying, 'This is the way; walk in it'" (Isaiah 30:21). As our spirit is free to feel His holy guidance, we realize His voice is already there. We just need to pause and listen.

At the beginning of the earth's existence, God was in the presence of Adam and Eve. They spoke with Him and heard His voice clearly. Their connection with God was ever present. Ours can be too. "My sheep listen to my voice; I know them, and they follow me" (John 10:27). A close relationship with Christ allows us to hear Him clearly. The distractions and attacks of our busy lives attempt to veer us off the straight path and deafen our spiritual ears. When Adam and Eve listened to the serpent, not God, it did not end well. We are all distracted at times. As I walk this journey, I see I am relearning lessons He already taught me. I am a slow learner but eager to step out in faith.

In this process, I remembered the different voices we can hear amid the busyness of life. We know we can hear God's voice. But we also hear our own voice, the words of our past, and the noise from the enemy. Satan speaks the opposite of God. When the chatter begins in our spirits, we have to discern the difference between God and Satan.

| | |
|---|---|
| Satan confuses. | God enlightens. |
| Satan pushes. | God leads. |
| Satan rushes. | God stills. |
| Satan worries. | God comforts. |
| Satan obsesses. | God calms. |
| Satan frightens. | God reassures. |
| Satan condemns. | God convicts. |

Discerning the voices leads to us understanding God's guidance so we can deny the voices of the flesh and of the enemy. It is not always as distinct as this. A spiritual push-and-pull happens in our souls. Confusion causes chaos. We push our way into decisions and work in our abilities. God pulls us with His guidance. Pushing our way rather than being pulled by God leads us to an inferior path.

Discerning God's higher thoughts guides us to walk in His higher ways.

*"For my thoughts are not your thoughts, neither are your ways my ways," declares the* Lord. *"As the heavens are higher than the earth, so are my ways higher than your ways and my thoughts than your thoughts."*

—Isaiah 55:8–9

A discerning spirit leads to confidence in God's guidance, making us more aware of our thoughts or the words of the enemy.

As children of God, we have confidence in being led by His Spirit. When our lives are in line, connecting fully with the Lord, we hear His guidance. "Whoever has ears, let them hear" (Matthew 13:9). We are able. How do we continue to connect with Jesus to listen? Draw nearer to Him.

"Be still, and know that I am God" (Psalm 46:10). How many times have we seen this Scripture on a placard at the Christian bookstore? Has your pastor said these words? Have you heard them in your Bible study group? Yes, we have all heard these words. But how easy is it to be obedient to them? God's "still" is the stillness related to our spirits. Believe you can hear Him. Expect to hear His voice within your spirit. Doubt decreases our ability to understand; confidence clears the connection. Connection glorifies God.

For six months during the baseball season, we live in an apartment in the city where my husband's team calls home. Packing up the apartment to go back to our actual home at the end baseball season gets me out of my usual routine of reading my Bible, praying, and listening to God's voice. It surprises me every year how much we accumulate in six months. The busyness of my life increases, and time with God decreases. "We must pay the most careful attention, therefore, to what we have heard, so that we do not drift away" (Hebrews 2:1). Boxing up all the accumulated junk takes up the time and space I should give to God, adding to the stuff that clutters the free spaces in my soul.

I make a pact with myself each year to not be so busy and overwhelmed when I get back home. I plan days of relaxation in a quiet spot to read or watch a movie. It never seems to happen. I always hit the ground running as soon as I get back home.

One year, when the season finally ended and everything was packed, I drove home to an empty house, alone. The early return was planned to help with the reentry into our off-season life. On the ride, I asked myself what had changed. I was anxious and confused, misdirected, and misguided. I felt disconnected from God.

In desperation to connect deeper with God, I planned a shutdown—a mental and to-do list shutdown. I texted my husband and our three boys and informed them as of midnight I would be off the grid for 24 hours. My intentions were spoken and set in stone. I would not be busy for the next 24 hours. I would be still. With good intentions, the shutdown was needed and meaningful.

Shutting down our busyness is not always the answer. No matter how few things I do, my brain doesn't stop. My thoughts swirl from one topic to another. Taking control of our minds and our spirits is integral to being still.

Early in our relationship, my husband would get irritated with me when I asked him what he was thinking. He'd reply, "Nothing," every time. He didn't get irritated with the question but rather with my reaction to his response.

"What do you mean, you are thinking of nothing? Can you even do that?" My mind never shuts down, much like my talking. I am constantly thinking, debating, questioning, answering, wondering, learning, negating. Always on. Always thinking. The concept of thinking about nothing doesn't exist in my world. Change had to happen.

Being still took work for me. Ironically, I was thinking about not thinking. I knew I had to learn to be still in my thoughts. I read about meditation and some strange concepts on enlightenment, but these didn't lead to the stillness God wanted. It would take discipline and new habits to learn to be still in my spirit in order to hear God speak. Each of us may execute this differently.

I closed my eyes and called His name. *Jesus.* Each time a thought of something else would peek through, I would say His name. *Jesus.* I set a timer for five minutes to sit in His presence. *Jesus.* It took practice, but over time I learned to be still. The more disciplined I became, the easier it was to be still even in the chaos of driving, traveling, people, and noise. *Jesus.* As you know, I am a slow learner of discipline; I have to remind myself each day to focus on being still. A scheduled discipline becomes a spiritual blessing.

I have talked about how prayer draws us closer to the awareness of God and understanding His will. Prayer is a daily conversation with Jesus. It isn't just a list of needs and desires but a part of our spirit, our relationship with Christ. As our relationship deepens with Christ, His Spirit actively works in us as our conversations increase with Him. Through our prayers, the Holy Spirit responds to us in our spirits.

Ask Him to speak to you, "God, what do You want to say to me?" In conversations with God, His presence becomes more real. "Call to me and I will answer you and tell you great and unsearchable things you do not know" (Jeremiah 33:3). God loves to talk to us. Make a request; ask Him to speak.

Samuel was in his mother Hannah's womb when she dedicated his life to the Lord. Then when he was a young child, Hannah took him to the sanctuary where the priest, Eli, raised him. Eli was responsible for Samuel's spiritual and religious training. One night as he slept, Samuel heard someone call his name. He went to see Eli. The priest must need something. But Eli hadn't called him. After Samuel heard the voice and went to Eli two more times, Eli understood it was God.

> So Eli told Samuel, "Go and lie down, and if he calls you, say, 'Speak, LORD, for your servant is listening.'" So Samuel went and lay down in his place. The LORD came and stood there, calling as at the other times, "Samuel! Samuel!" Then Samuel said, "Speak, for your servant is listening." And the LORD said to Samuel: "See, I am about to do something in Israel that will make the ears of everyone who hears about it tingle."
>
> —1 Samuel 3:9–11

Ask God to speak. Let's be part of something that when others hear, their ears tingle. Pray and ask. Speak, God, for Your servant is listening.

God's Word is living and active. He speaks to us every day through Scripture. Reading the Bible connects us to God's guidance by understanding the way He speaks. We get to know how He has talked to others and how He can speak to us. We know we are supposed to read His Word. Sometimes it just doesn't happen.

Remember that quiet corner with a cup of tea, my Bible, and a blanket? It rarely happens. When the kids were young, quiet time didn't exist. A cup of hot black coffee for a burst of energy was a blessing. As they grew older, I filled my extra time with what I thought were "good Christian" activities, including Bible study. Nothing can replace reading the Bible, God's breathed words.

I don't know how time with God looks for you. I have to be purposeful to sit down with my Bible some days. To open it and pray for a new and fresh perspective. To absorb His words in my soul.

My 24-hour shutdown began slowly. To-dos raged for attention in my head. I prayed for God to calm my mind and remind me of all the things I was afraid I would forget to do. My thoughts slowed my heartbeat in a pattern of peace and comfort. I grabbed my Bible and began to read. Again my mind ran away from the words I was reading. I prayed for the Lord to make His Word new and fresh to my mind and for Him to guide me.

God has given us a spirit of strength, power, love, and a sound mind. We have the ability to take our thoughts captive and have the strength to walk in the power of a sound mind.

I laid the Bible in front of me and wondered where to start. I closed it and asked God to speak to me. "Jesus, take me where You want me to read. Make Your Word fresh and new to me," I requested. I opened the Bible to Ephesians. What? Really? Ephesians is the book that started this whole adventure. So I questioned again what God was doing. If I was honestly going to find what more He desired for me, I had to obey. The title of Ephesians 2 in the New International Version is "Made Alive in Christ." Fresh and new? I'd read it before. My notes in the margin say my former pastor in Boston preached on it. There was nothing new about this passage.

But I stopped and prayed for a fresh and new look at His Word. I read verses 4–5, "But because of his great love for us, God, who is rich in mercy, made us alive with Christ even when we were dead in transgressions—it is by grace you have been saved." Tears rose in my eyes. "Not my abilities, Lord. But Your great love, mercy, and grace," I prayed. Oh, sweet Jesus spoke to me. No matter what I do or want to do, He has already accomplished more for me. Fresh and new! God's love for me has saved me from myself. He has accomplished this, wanting nothing in return.

God's Word is at work in us, transforming us as we read and learn. The Bible brings a newness and freshness to our spirits. Reading the Bible is not a duty; the spiritual connection to Jesus is a gift. From Scripture, we learn how He spoke to others. We become more aware of His direction. Ask Him to speak through His Word in a new and fresh way. Enjoy. God gave all of Scripture to us. Men wrote it, but He gave them the words. Scripture is for us to understand God and learn how to hear His voice in our lives. The Bible provides us with the filters to judge if we are hearing God. We discern ideas and thoughts with the words in the Bible. They are impressed on us by God.

*Therefore we do not lose heart. Though outwardly we are wasting away, yet inwardly we are being renewed day by day. For our light and momentary troubles are achieving for us an eternal glory that far outweighs them all. So we fix our eyes not on what is seen, but on what*

> *is unseen, since what is seen is temporary, but*
> *what is unseen is eternal.*
>
> —*2 Corinthians 4:16–18*

In the moments of asking God to make all things new, He does. He has made us new in our faith in Him. He makes His Word fresh each day when we reach out to absorb it.

Decreasing the busyness increases our connection with God. Can we take our schedule and thoughts captive and focus on connecting with Jesus? *Speak, Lord. Your servant is listening.*

I have read many stories of monks who spend their entire day meditating, reading God's Word, and praying. I wish I had monk time. In our busy lives, we have to be intentional in taking moments to be still, pray, ask, and read. Humbling ourselves to the almighty power of God during these moments deepens our relationship with Him and opens our spirits to hear His guidance.

Beginning our day with a prayer is an invitation for God to speak. With an intention to hear His voice when starting our day, we are expectant. As we take the time to listen in the first hours, we wait with an open heart. God manifests Himself to us as we humbly seek Him. "Trust in the Lord with all your heart and lean not on your own understanding; in all your ways submit to him, and he will make your paths straight" (Proverbs 3:5–6). The straight path to communication starts first thing in the morning. Wake, pray, and ask. The Holy Spirit will speak to you. Call out to Him.

Invite God to tell you what His desires are. I began to ask each day. *What is it You want me to do for You today, Lord?* Through the stillness of thoughts, His peace followed me through every circumstance and situation, guiding and leading me. In times when I couldn't hear Him speaking, I become anxious. Sometimes He doesn't speak immediately. Patience is a virtue—not one I like to rely on but a virtue nonetheless.

When desperate for answers or guidance, fasting from food or activities can help us break free of the outside distractions and busyness that clog the spiritual connection. In the Bible, people used fasting as a spiritual discipline. Jesus fasted for 40 days to help Him hear God (Matthew 4:2). In the Book of Acts, we see the apostles fasted to help them hear God's guidance (Acts 13:2). Fasting is part of our journey through life. It leads to a deeper devotion to prayer and spiritual connection. Self-denial trains us in submission.

Many people are detoxing and fasting from foods to become healthier. Detoxing and fasting to pray and meditate on God's Word and voice leads to a healthier connection to Christ. The benefits of detoxing from unhealthy items to make our bodies healthier are similar to spiritual detoxing.

People detox from certain foods for several reasons. It boosts energy and rids the body of excess waste. It helps with weight loss and strengthens the immune system. It promotes healthy changes, clears thinking, benefits antiaging, and improves a sense of well-being.

Detoxing of the busyness and distractions of our lives has similar benefits. It boosts our spiritual energy and rids us of the excess waste in our lives. The weight of the world is off our shoulders and left at the Cross. We stand firm. We release the feeling of the weight of the world on us. We are improved when we are in close relationship. Listening for God's guidance creates healthy changes and enhances Christlike thinking. We have eternal life. He has a plan for our lives.

We clear junk from our soul to open our connection with Christ. Continuing to purify our minds, lives, and souls keeps us open to God's guidance. A detox of the junk in our spirits leaves our ears ready to listen for His small whispers.

God's desire should be our ultimate goal. In each situation, when we listen for His guidance we listen to fulfill His wishes. Even if we don't feel we hear God's voice, we can proceed in faith, find peace in the decision, and move forward.

Understanding God's guidance is a spiritual discipline that becomes part of our spirit. Straining, in our own strength, to hear His voice will only close our spiritual ears. Trusting and believing God will speak opens our hearts to His guidance. As our relationship with Christ increases, our ability to hear also develops. We cannot force the process. Leaning in and growing closer expands our spiritual closeness. We make it our goal to become spiritually mature people.

Having a godly mentor or prayer partner helps to discern the different voices and hold them up to God's Word. Godly counsel and accountability is a safe place to share and learn. Without guidance, people fall. With a responsibility partner, we confirm facts together. Not worldly facts but truth and wisdom from God.

Please avoid the mistakes I made in my desperation to find a godly mentor. I went about it as I had many things in my Christian life—on my own. My abilities repeatedly fell short as I sought out who I thought would be a good mentor for me. The connections never happened. The women I chose were godly, wonderful women but were not the person God had chosen. After a few failed attempts, I went where I should have in the beginning—to Him. I prayed He would match me with the godly woman He had for me to pray with and live this adventure of life with, a disciple maker.

It didn't happen immediately, but in time, God paired me with the woman He wanted to use to guide and lead me, and I her. We talk and pray weekly. If we cannot talk, we touch base. Times of desperation sometimes happen just after we hang up. When I need godly counsel in those times, I know I can send a message, and we connect. We use text, email, or social media to connect and lead each other back to hearing God's voice, not others', the enemy's, or our own.

Our time together is well spent. We share what we are struggling with, what we desire, and what we are praying for. While our conversations may begin by venting our struggles, hardships, and needs, we always turn to God, His Word, and prayer. A prayer partner or mentor is one who holds you accountable to God's Word, not the world's view.

*Let the message about Christ, in all its richness, fill your lives. Teach and counsel each other with all the wisdom he gives. Sing psalms and hymns and spiritual songs to God with thankful hearts.*

*—Colossians 3:16 NLT*

We don't sing to one another (I wouldn't do that to anyone); however, when we finish talking my heart sings praises for the time we spent together seeking God's guidance, wisdom, and desires.

In Exodus, when God commanded the Israelites to go from place to place, they questioned if God was with them. Then the Amalekites attacked them. Moses told Joshua to go and fight. Moses stood on top of the hill with the staff in his hand lifted to God. Aaron and Hur went up the hill with him. As long as Moses had the staff in the air, the Amalekites were defeated. When he lowered his hand, the Israelites lost.

*When Moses' hands grew tired, they took a stone and put it under him and he sat on it. Aaron and Hur held his hands up—one on one side, one on the other—so his hands remained steady till sunset. So Joshua overcame the Amalekite army with the sword.*

*—Exodus 17:12–13*

Choose the people you surround yourself with wisely. Who is helping you hold up your arms? Surrounding yourself with godly friends helps support your obedience to God.

As my heart made more and more room for God to move, I needed to share what I had learned with others. I talked with friends. I was vulnerable and honest about my shortcomings and the growth I was seeing through this process of decreasing busyness and increasing my awareness of what God wants to do in and through me. The presence of others and their ability to encourage me took my journey to an entirely new level. Linking arms with godly women helps our spirit and deepens our faith. Grab a group of three or four friends to link arms in this journey. Have some tea, and sit and talk a while. Share your struggles and concerns. Lift each other's arms when you need a stronger spirit.

Much to my chagrin, I have realized God will remain silent if it is not yet in His time to reveal an answer to you. It may not be this side of heaven, and we may never know. Just remember: God's ways are better than any way we could try to pave for ourselves. I once told our pastor I could not wait to be face-to-face with Jesus so I could get the answers to the questions I hadn't received yet from the Lord. He said, "When you are face-to-face with Jesus it won't matter anymore. His presence will be enough." The statement sank into my heart. I knew some questions might never be answered, and it didn't matter. His plan is better than anything I could dream of happening. Glorifying Him while I wait to hear is my goal.

*God can do anything, you know—far more than you could ever imagine or guess or request in your wildest dreams! He does it not by pushing us around but by working within us, his Spirit deeply and gently within us. Glory to God in the church! Glory to God in the Messiah, in Jesus!*

> *Glory down all the generations! Glory through all*
> *millennia! Oh yes!*
> —*Ephesians 3:20–21 The Message*

We have been created to glorify God. I walk through this journey and continue to embrace what God is doing in me each and every day. The work God has done creates joy and desire to live a life that represents the sacrifice Jesus made on the Cross. But my journey was still not complete. It was just the beginning of His desire to work through my actions—not adding to the to-do list but focusing my commitment to Him. Our lives are an example of what Christ has done for us. He gave His life for the forgiveness of our sins. Jesus came to walk on earth as a man, to give us life so we could live to the fullest. With our awareness of His Spirit, understanding His will, and now hearing His guidance, we are ready to move on to what He wants to do through us.

Being still, taking thoughts captive, and submitting them to God is a daily battle. Listening to Him guides our thoughts in a deeper connection. This adventure continued to build as I searched for more.

PART 3 | Exploring the Ways God Wants to Work through Us

# *Intentional Living*

## CHAPTER SEVEN

As my journey continued, I realized God's desire in a new way. My life actions had to change because of the deepening connection I was experiencing with Christ. It was like a bubbling fountain alive inside of my spirit, ready to flow. I had new intentions and motivation to purposefully live to glorify God.

The transformation wasn't complete in my soul, but the pull of God to keep moving was strong. While we focus on what God is doing *in* us, we are focused on *ourselves*. Moving into intentional living is a natural progression to outwardly glorifying *Him*.

The deepening connection with Jesus throughout the journey filled my spirit with the need to serve God. I began to wonder when God would move in my life. When will He tell me my purpose? What am I meant to do? We have to be careful that these moments of pausing don't turn us into potato chip Christians who lie back on the couch, eat one chip at a time, and wait for the Lord to send down some thunderbolt of knowledge with a big-screen view of our future, purpose, and meaning.

A stagnant life for a Christian begins when we wait without movement. Forward motion, the first step of belief and trust, living the life God has given us, keeps our sights on glorifying God where we are. Walking into potential rather than staying stuck in the quagmire.

Intentional living is living life on purpose. A deliberate, by-design, determined life lived for the glory of God. Living an intentional life leads to remarkable living. We need to be willing to make an effort for our behavior to reflect our beliefs.

Coming together with like-minded people forms intentional communities. The group of friends we can join with to hold each of us accountable becomes a remarkable group of God-glorifying people. We learn from each other as we seek the extraordinary life God desires. We emulate the joyful lives of those around us. Friends who help you become more Christlike every day are friends who live to glorify God. Have you found a few women to walk with in this season of adventure? Are you praying for a few women to hold up your arms when you get tired?

Intentional living moves us from stagnant existence to the significant life intended for us. It focuses on glorifying God in a relationship with Jesus and deepens our faith, hope, and love. It places us face-to-face with Jesus every day.

The gospel has an effect on us in character, development, maturity, and behavior. The transformation happens through our connection with the Holy Spirit. We are a work in progress. We have a responsibility to represent the gospel and the effect it will have on others. We must choose to live a "whatever" life (Philippians 4:8), wherever He desires to have a gospel influence.

A gospel influence is allowing the gospel to penetrate the places we play, live, and work. In permitting the gospel into these areas, we have to allow it to guide all our actions. We will never be perfect, but we need to live our lives in relation to God's power, not our own.

We have a responsibility in how we represent our relationship with Christ. We are human. We sin. We will never be perfect and may be judged wrongly, but we cannot let sin stop us. Be filled with the Holy Spirit. Patterning our lives after Jesus leads us to have this influence. What is the result? God's glory is put on display.

Life, as I have known it in the past, was extremely self-focused. I have been humbled by how God directed my steps even though I was not seeking His guidance in different seasons of my life.

I recently attended my thirtieth high school reunion, and it caused me to reflect on all the things I pursued in high school. My life was self-focused. What do I want to be when I grow up? Where do I want to go to college? What will be my major? Who will I date and later marry? What will be my lifelong career? It was all me and very little God.

Reflecting on my past showed me the many layers I had to peel away over my lifetime. I was reminded of the layers of an onion I chose to use in a recipe for dinner. It had a very thick skin. With the top cut off, I peeled the exterior, revealing the outer layer of the white onion. There was a rotten piece on one side of the outer layer. Peeling it back, I saw the rot went farther than I had seen before. I continued to peel back the decay until I reached a place of wholeness. The same happens in our travel through our spiritual transformation.

God reveals a blemish in our souls the same way. He chisels the decay away. Our spirit looks like it is in good shape. Then He reveals another piece in need of removal. What more did God want to do in me? I wasn't a complete project. Our spiritual lives are continually refined in order to reveal His work.

We often become focused on ourselves even though we believe in God's mighty existence. We must be purposefully focused on what God is calling us to do outside of ourselves. We can't live the potato chip Christian life of sitting and waiting until God finishes all the work in us before we begin to allow Him to work through us. We must move forward even if we don't have a clear view of what lies ahead.

The changes God was doing in me created a desire to serve Him in a deeper way. God wants to use us to accomplish what only He can do. Being a believer in Christ, we are given power by God to be able to achieve the work He has set before us. It is the same strength God used when He raised Jesus from the dead. What an almighty power we have at our disposal.

We get lost when we focus on our purpose and the meaning of our lives rather than God's purpose and meaning. It is not only what God can do for us but also what we can do for God. Now. In this place. At this time. One choice at a time. As I continued to reflect, God challenged me more. I asked the Lord, "What do You want me to do for You today?"

I made a choice to begin my intentional living. I was making a move from the robotic—following the everyday chores and checklists—to living for Jesus on purpose.

I hate when I call a company only to hear a robotic voice. The voice lists different departments or different issues you may be having, along with the corresponding number to press in order to go to that department or have that particular issue resolved. The only problem is sometimes none of the options answers the question I need answered. Yelling into the phone changes nothing. I just want to speak to a human! Then I press 0, as if it might take me to a human, only to be prompted back to the beginning of the menu.

No, I do not want to live in a world of robots. I want human interaction and choices. The balance comes when we seek the Lord's guidance. We choose to cleanse our spirits, become aware of God's presence, understand His will, and listen for His guidance. He doesn't put us on hold, nor does He forward our call to an automated service.

We cannot control many things in life, but we can seek to glorify God in all that we say, do, and are. Attitudes and decisions from our past do not have to dictate who we are now or in our future. They can influence decisions, but they do not define who we are. Our choices can change from detrimental to beneficial in a split second.

Relying on God is necessary when we make decisions. Life is made up of these choices. As I grow closer to Christ, events from my past seem to rear their ugly heads. Beware of the attacks. They don't only happen in initial stages of life. They can occur in every step we take. We can decide to allow them to overwhelm us or we can choose to stand strong on the promises of God's helping hand. Waiting for the perfect time or circumstance wastes the opportunity to live a remarkable life. We can decide to live with regrets and hurts of the past or step forward in faith to live life to the fullest. God has given us life to live to the fullest. Accept the gift.

Choices form our decisions. We judge the value of the decision based on our beliefs. We can choose from multiple options. We make simple choices without much thought of their outcome. More complex decisions are made by choice. Having a choice is seen as a positive option until we become confused about what is best or what is meant to be.

Not every idea is God-appointed. With God's guidance in understanding His will, we can make informed decisions to glorify Him in our choices. Looking at the outcomes of each decision in light of the sacrifice Christ made for us leads us to a choice that is godly.

We cannot blame our lives and circumstances on past experiences, whether good or bad. This becomes especially problematic when we let the past have total control over us and paralyze our decision making. It is better to take responsibility and make decisions based on God's biblical guidance for our lives, choosing to live a life that is gospel-centered and Jesus-focused. Be careful not to do what sounds good to you but what God is leading you to in your decision and plan.

This often leads us to doing what we can where we can. Sometimes we are led to work in our neighborhoods . . . or even in our homes. Men and women who chose to live with intention have changed the world. Consider Bob Pierce. He once wrote in his Bible, "Let my heart be broken with the things that break the heart of God." Bob's heart for God led him to found World Vision International, and in 1970, Samaritan's Purse. Both organizations serve those in need and have a worldwide impact. Asking God to break our hearts for what breaks His opens our spirits to experience the life God desires for each of us. Be bold. Pray for a new perspective of our intentional life.

Knowing God works for the good of those who believed, I took a chance. The prayer was on shaky knees. It was more of a question of a question. I wondered if I should even ask. "God, what do You want me to do for You?" The condemning thoughts that riddled my mind diminished my bold prayer. I asked again more boldly, ready for guidance. He answered, slowly revealing the layers of what I needed at that time. I had a sense of responsibility to serve "the least of these" but didn't know what that meant in my life. I prayed again, asking God for His desires. "Beloved, if our hearts do not condemn us, we have boldness before God" (1 John 3:21 NRSV). He answered by revealing more. It wasn't a complete plan but a peaceful response. Then the suggestions riddled me.

The first happened when I was preparing dinner for my family and a local television station aired a special report on adoption day in our city. They made an appeal to their viewers to respond for the city's intense need for foster homes. The number of children in need far exceeded the foster families available. Soon after we received a flier in the mail that stated more than 8,000 children were in our local foster care system. Approximately 2,500 children were identified as released for adoption. There were 5,500 children in need of a temporary place to stay while they were waiting for permanent placement. My heart felt burdened after reading James 1:27. I had always dreamed of going to a foreign country, but at that moment I knew God wanted me to serve in my backyard, to serve the children who were in need of a loving home.

Intentional living begins with a decision to change the way we see service. We serve those in need out of the love that God has given us. We are guided by God's Word and are pursuing godly character. When we see our purpose is to live for the glory of God, more opportunities present themselves. Each day we have to be willing to take the next step.

My next prayer was selfish but heartfelt, "God, if You don't want me to pursue this, then shut the doors and the windows and, and, and . . ." The thought and urging of fostering frightened me. I talked with my husband and children about this urging. As a family, we prayed for God's guidance. We took a step of faith, knowing the urging was from God but not knowing what the future held. Intentional living emerges when we choose to step out in faith and serve.

We decided to pursue foster care. We believed we could bless these children during their time of instability. I can tell you now the future held more blessings than we could have ever imagined. There were a lot of bumps and bruises through the process, but fostering the three babies we had over a three-year period solidified the belief that God has a plan better than anything we could ever imagine. The blessings we received outweighed the blessings we ever gave. Funny how God turns what we think is blessing others into a whole new perspective on our faith.

When heading into the empty nest, I began to pray about what my next role in life would be. I had been a full-time, stay-at-home mom for 20 years after a nursing career. I was mother and wife, an identity I loved with all my heart. There was a mourning period during my youngest son's senior year of high school.

I decided to volunteer to help my friend, Katharine, test a book she was writing: *Write a Novel in Ten Minutes a Day*. I would be part of a group that would read the book, complete the exercises and offer feedback. I learned a lot during those months. I felt God pulling me in the direction of taking my writing seriously, something He had spoken into my spirit ten years before. I hadn't listened.

Fears and negative thoughts kept me from hearing and obeying God's call. I stopped living a deliberate, by design, determined life. The first step in my writing journey started in 2005 when I published my first devotion on Baseball Chapel's website. I chose only to write what I was comfortable with, rather than fully committing to what God was asking of me. I didn't accept His guidance. After writing for ten years, I still didn't consider myself a writer, even though God did. I felt that I wrote the devotions but someone else edited and made them look good. They took less commitment and risk.

Doing the writing exercises for my friend catapulted my desire to write and decreased my fear. I began to blog and learn more about the writing process. Another friend who had published a book agreed to talk with me and mentor me in my future writing endeavors. I made tangible goals and went to my first writer's conference.

My first conference was met with a lot of rejection from publishers. I was building my platform, but everything seemed to be falling short. But I continued to stick to the goals I made and took them one by one. My strength was failing, and my disappointments were stacking up. A gentle nudge in my spirit urged me to pray. I prayed for God to confirm my calling. He confirmed I needed to do the next thing and not get caught up in the bigger picture.

Little by little I did the next thing. I made daily and weekly goals. I achieved some of them. I reevaluated the ones that didn't get met. I just did the next thing. I went where God pulled. When I was attending my second writer's conference, I verbally confirmed to others, and myself: I am a writer!

God asked me to allow Him to pull me where He wanted me to go, not push what I was intent on conquering. There were unachievable goals written, but I dreamed and prayed for His guidance. I did the next thing He pulled me toward in His power. I had to choose to be purposeful in my journey. There were dreams even I couldn't dream or think were possible.

My knowledge and power are limited. God's are not. Stand boldly in front of a great God who is always at work. He desires us to stand before Him and be courageous (Joshua 1:9). We shouldn't underestimate the power of His work. We only need to believe to receive this power.

One of my favorite Bible verses is Luke 1:38, which says, "'I am the Lord's servant,' Mary answered. 'May your word to me be fulfilled.' Then the angel left her." We all know the story. The beautiful introduction to Jesus—the Savior of the world. The angel Gabriel came to Mary and informed her she was highly favored. She was frightened. If being visited by an angel wasn't frightening enough, he proceeded to tell her she was going to become pregnant even though she was a virgin. I know I would have been freaked out. *What will people think? How on earth could this happen? Poor Joseph.*

Mary, much wiser than I, listened. Then Gabriel told her how it would be. The translation of the verse that most intrigues me is, "'For every promise from God shall surely come true.' Mary said, 'I am the Lord's servant, and I am willing to do whatever he wants. May everything you said come true.' And then the angel disappeared" (Luke 1:37–38 TLB). When Mary listened to Gabriel, she moved from being the Lord's servant to living an intentional "whatever" life—whatever God wants. To live a whatever life became my desire. Scripture guided me to the way to begin this type of life.

Do whatever God tells us to do. Do the next thing. With this spiritual journey, our spirit is ready to allow God to work through us. After the death of Moses, his aid Joshua was commanded by God to lead the people of Israel. "Then they answered Joshua, 'Whatever you have commanded us we will do, and wherever you send us we will go'" (Joshua 1:16). Doing whatever God wants wherever He wants is living an intentional life.

Each December, I write a list of goals for the following year. Remember, I like lists, and I am a work in progress. My lists have been shallow and me-focused in the past. Now I have to question what the focus of my goals should be. We have learned to be bold in front of the Lord. To live a whatever life wherever God wants, my focus shifts from what I want and think I need to allowing Jesus to fill my spirit with His desires. Jesus' desire is for His glory to be put on display while spreading the gospel.

A cost comes along with living an intentional life and using gospel influence. While at a conference, I heard David Platt speak about our need to put a blank check on the table of our lives. Again the need to say, "Here I am." *Whatever. Wherever.* He said to then let God fill in the check, a seemingly dangerous suggestion. The danger is surrendering your life and submitting to His will. The cost is fulfilling His call on your life. Our purpose is to glorify Him in all that we say, do, and are. Whatever. Whenever.

"That person is like a tree planted by streams of water, which yields its fruit in season and whose leaf does not wither—whatever they do prospers" (Psalm 1:3). A whatever life believes in the Almighty God, stands in awe of the Resurrection, and advances His kingdom. Our lives prosper by glorifying Him and knowing He is our reward. Our purpose, our meaning in life should circle back each and every time to the glory of God.

The adventure of seeking to serve and glorify God can only happen when we are spiritually connected. Our spiritual lives need to be nurtured and fed each day in order to continue understanding His will and pursuing His guidance. Allowing God to work in us on a continual basis cultivates a spirit that is willing and able to serve and glorify God.

Focusing on intentional living reveals moments of significance— holy, impactful moments. Intentional living is living our lives each and every day to represent Christ, serving Him through our actions and words. Ask the Lord to reveal the opportunities to help others. When we ask for Him to expose these possibilities, God lays them out very clearly before us. But do we choose to listen to or see what He has shown us?

When you feel the urge to pray for someone, pray. When God nudges you to talk with someone, talk. When a friend needs to vent, listen. Be purposeful, focusing on these urgings from God. Stop and obey. When we live with intention to glorify God, our paths are made straight; His power works.

Early in my life, I knew without question that God created me to do good works. "Before I made you in your mother's womb, I chose you. Before you were born, I set you apart for a special work" (Jeremiah 1:5 NCV). As I entertained living a whatever life, I realized I was focused on the work part and not the *special* work idea. The work God calls us to do is not the busy kind that bogs us down with stress and anxiety trying to represent Him. It is the kind of work laced with love and used to glorify Him, to help others as if serving Him personally.

One result of living intentionally within God's will for your life will be a change in attitude toward serving Him as well as His children. A conscious effort to understand what is going on around us allows us to see the need. Are we feeding the hungry and the thirsty and serving strangers? Hunger makes us think of serving in a soup kitchen or buying a homeless person a meal, but hunger and thirst can also refer to spiritual hunger. Pouring God's Word and living water out for others to be filled is serving those who may not receive it otherwise. Strangers in our lives can be our neighbors and even our family. Those individuals could be people who rub us the wrong way, not fitting into the comfortable life we want among the busyness of our lives. Sometimes we don't have time to serve those people.

If we begin to see serving others as if we are serving Christ Himself, it becomes a service of love. Many times in my past I have not served with this kind of love. I thought serving made me look like a good person, a hard worker, a good Christian. It was all about me, not God. Once I began to prioritize seeking God and allowing Him to work through me, I saw the amazing things He could accomplish when I allowed Him to work in me and do His work through me. I stopped thinking about me and started to think about serving "the least of these."

Another pitfall was I would choose who I thought was most needy or most worthy. I would turn down opportunities to serve because I felt certain people did not deserve the service they were getting. Again, the conviction of Matthew 25:35–40 changed my desire to serve all. The blessing I was receiving, in seeking God's guidance in my life, was freely given by God. Shouldn't I do the same to others by giving without questioning their value? Serving others guides us to the right places, organizations, street corners, and homeless shelters and to opening a door for someone, holding a door for a mom with a stroller, smiling at the checkout clerk, and on.

Knowing God has set us apart to do special works gives us the confidence to serve others in His name, bringing generous blessings. And in every instance of helping others, the blessings are not just for them. We walk away blessed beyond measure. The forward movement in faith and commitment to obey God's desire for us to live an intentional life relies on His strength and power.

Making sure we get our spiritual supply from prayer and God's Word gives us sustenance to propel God's gospel influence. Filling our spirit with Him, pouring the excess out to others, allows moments of significance.

Each day we have an opportunity to allow such moments. Daily touches are opportunities I learned early in my season of motherhood. For example, when your child walks into a room, you may be tempted to blow him or her off. You just need five minutes to yourself. What would happen if every time you saw your child, you lit up with joy? It is not easy when we are angry or don't want to express joy, but our children need to see the love we have for them and the joy we feel just because they exist. This is a daily touch.

For me, showing joy was a bit arduous. Staying home with my children while my husband traveled extensively was hard. I was often tired and in desperate need for some quiet. But the results of those daily touches on my children's lives proved the quiet I thought I needed could wait a little longer.

A daily touch also helps us evaluate our priorities of serving others. It helps to assess not what we are doing but why we are doing it. Are we doing things that benefit only us? Is it about what God desires or what we desire? Our desire to seek an opportunity for those daily touches in others' lives is purposeful living. Shining His love to others while continuing to trust God when and where he calls us.

When I chose to make it a priority to light up every time one of my children walked into the room, I saw joy in my boys' faces. I felt just as much joy. I began to think how this would change my husband's reaction when he approached me. I would light up when he approached me; his joy was radiant. All from a simple daily touch. We will forget at times. However, when we make intentionally touching others' lives a priority, it makes a difference. The same happens when you offer a daily touch to strangers, friends, acquaintances, workers, cashiers . . . just about anyone you come in contact with.

"Love one another. As I have loved you" (John 13:34) is a command from Jesus. If every day we go out with the intention to reveal what the Lord is doing in us by looking for a way we can have a daily touch in the lives of others, we love as Christ loves us. The special work God has set us apart to do may not be something earth-shattering at this season of our life. He wants you to do a special work in your classroom, coffee shop job, marriage, friendships, daily interactions, or wherever you may be in this season of your life.

Another moment of significance God commands us to participate in is tithing. Tithing is a difficult topic for many, at one time myself included. It is very uncomfortable to visit a church and hear about their need for money. The heart of tithing, not the duty or guilt, is what God seeks from us.

Money is a major topic in the Bible and is mentioned more than 800 times. We are called to give off the top of all the money we make. Let me restate that. We are called to give off the top of all God gives us! God provides us the ability to have the money we earn and receive. The money is His first. He calls us to give from the money we have been given.

My husband and I had some hard times financially over the years. We thought we needed the money more than our home church needed it. After hearing a few great speakers on the topic of money and our responsibility to tithe, our hearts began to change.

In the Book of Mark, we read a story about a poor widow who gave even though she lived in poverty (Mark 12:41–44). I questioned my reluctance to give. She had given *all* of what she had to the Lord. But how could she? How would she live? She sought God's kingdom first. She believed in obedience. She would give, and God would take care of what she would eat, drink, and wear. She didn't worry. Her story is a beautiful picture of intentional living.

She had faith like no other. She believed God would provide for her. *May I have faith like that, Lord?* Mine and Dave's hearts and attitudes began to change. We began to tithe and give out of obedience and faith. And our lives changed. No, we did not have a massive windfall of money, but a significant change was made in our hearts. We do not tithe out of a sense of duty or guilt but out of faith knowing God is the one who has given us the money. We are to give back to Him through our church.

Tithing is like the training wheels of faith. The lessons of respecting money begin with tithing. It is important to God and to us that we are responsible with money. To tithe brings about a heart change. Our responsibility to God about our money becomes more important. We stop serving two masters with our obsession with money. We cannot serve God and money.

Freeing up the space that love and concern of money engulfed in us allowed more room to glorify Jesus. As our faith grew and our finances were in control, we saw we had more opportunities to give over and beyond our tithes. First, we tithe to our church. Then we can give to other ministries we feel God has led us to support.

Giving is such a blessing. The money God has entrusted us with becomes a great support to ministries and has been of part of serving God all over the world. Becoming a giving family has increased our faith and our love of giving.

Purposeful living through our service to others and with our finances is the initial action that God desires to do through us. Remarkable living is intentional obedience to God. Intentional living is pleasing to God. His blessings flow out to us in our purposeful pursuit of the immeasurably more He desires to do through our lives.

Let's put those potato chips down, get off the couch, and seek a deliberate, by design, determined life lived for the glory of God.

# Platform

## CHAPTER EIGHT

After a renowned speaker had completed her talk, my friends and I discussed a feeling deep in our spirits, agreeing we all wanted what she had. We wanted the presence she had on the stage. The way she held the audience captive was fascinating. She presented God's Word in a way that inflated our spirit and faith. Her presentation was smooth and intriguing, building desires in each woman present to serve God in a whole new way. As my friends and I approached her, we overheard another woman express the exact thoughts we discussed at our table. The speaker's response deflated our hopes like a slowly leaking balloon.

She said God made us all individuals who would be called to do the specific thing God had called us to do. She went on to say it might be speaking on a large stage in front of thousands of women, but we needed to start where God had us at that moment, embracing the opportunities He had for us then and there.

I don't think any of us wanted to start where we were—at home with little kids and no time to create anything new. We all had a burning desire to serve in a grand way. We wanted what she had, and we wanted it right then. (I told you, I am a work in progress.)

I had no tangible platform. I was a stay-at-home mom. The majority of my time was busy with kids' activities. I was too busy to be reaching out to others. These were some of the thoughts I had. Over time I have heard these and more excuses in different seasons of others' lives. We have a platform because we are children of God, not because of any performance-based popularity.

God gives us all a platform, an area where He places us to show His glory through us. Our unique platform is to be used to display all of God's glory, revealing what He desires to do through us.

In today's culture, we hear a lot of buzz about having a platform. The belief is we have to build it if we have any desire to influence others. It is is easy to believe that the people with the biggest platform have the most significant impact. Having a large platform reaches more people, yes. But does it reach the individuals with the message we are called to spread? Is this God's intention? Is it just one more item on our to-do list?

I was at a juncture in my life. Empty nest was impending. I would have lots of extra time on my hands. I once again read the Scripture that started this journey, "Now to him who is able to do immeasurably more than all we ask or imagine, according to his power that is at work within us" (Ephesians 3:20).

With all we have learned during this spiritual journey, we know the need to return to Him with every breath, clinging to His power at work within us. We cannot go forward in our power and expect Him to do what we want, how we want it. When we allow Him to guide and lead, pulling us into His desires and will, He is able to do more than we could ever imagine. Our desire to serve God in a grand way is the motivation to relinquish to His power within us.

Our platform begins where we are standing, sitting, bending, lifting, hugging, loving, and learning. When we surrender to God, we start to see He has created and equipped us to glorify Him. We display God's glory because of who He is.

As I surrendered to God, He continued to pull me toward writing. Slowly I increased the devotions I submitted to Baseball Chapel.

I stood alongside a writer friend in her journey, and I started to regularly blog. I continued to learn the craft and needs of the profession, but doubts and fears continued to plague me.

But that fear subsided as God continually confirmed I was to write. I began to chase the platform I was told the publishing houses coveted. I wrote goals and hunted down followers. I took classes online on how to increase my numbers. The problem was I became hyper-focused on building the platform publishers wanted and neglected the calling God had given me—to write.

Listening to others about how to increase my influence became more important than listening to God and His guidance. I was falling to idolatry, looking to man to give what only God could. God-built influences focus on the love of God. We can do all sorts of things to increase the number of people or opportunities to impact others for Christ, but we are not advancing the gospel, letting others in on the amazing love of Christ, without letting God place us where He wants us.

I have struggled over the years with where God wanted to use me. When I was a new Christian, I wanted to make an impact for God's kingdom. I wanted others to know about the amazing grace of Christ. How could I have influence for Christ? Life doesn't always fall into place the way we think it should.

Pride is the root of comparison and creates a temptation to desire what others have. Our culture teaches us that when we feel less than others, we need to focus on ourselves more to create a better outcome. Paul tells us a different story in 1 Corinthians. Paul says he doesn't judge himself. He doesn't care what others think about him. Looking to others and what they expect leads to despair. Social pressure leads to attempting to live up to others' standards. We want an unwavering sense of work that is unshakable. Our sense of identity comes from looking upward not inward.

*For who makes you different from anyone else? What do you have that you did not receive? And if you did receive it, why do you boast as though you did not?*

—*1 Corinthians 4:7*

All we have we have received from Christ. We cannot boast or feel despair if we have rooted our existence in the one who gives freely. Flee from the endless quest of what the world sees as a successful platform. God has made a way He desires for us.

My husband is a very quiet man who doesn't use a lot of words unless he is in his comfort zone—a baseball clubhouse and dugout. Then he is very animated and purposeful in his job setting. When we go to a gathering with a large number of strangers, he will be found in a back corner observing the crowd. I, on the other hand, am just the opposite. If we go to a gathering of 500 people, I will make sure I talk with at least 495 before I leave. I am the last in our family to leave church on Sunday mornings. I chat with anyone who makes eye contact with me. My comfort zone is in large crowds. Things haven't changed since elementary school.

One would think with the gift of gab God has given me, I would be in a profession that takes lots of time talking with people and building relationships. In my former career, this was true. I was a nurse and spent many hours talking to patients and their families. Then God called me to be a stay-at-home mom. I had a lot of time at home, alone, with three little boys. We moved a lot, and I didn't have a chance to make meaningful new friendships outside of my husband's work.

My husband's career took him in an entirely opposite direction of his personality. He is a professional baseball coach and works in front of 20,000–60,000 people on most game nights. He is comfortable because he doesn't have to talk with them all. He stays in the dugout and only talks with players and coaches. But as an MLB coach, my husband is asked on occasion to speak in front of large crowds.

Many teams in the MLB have one night a year when they have Faith Night. After the game, coaches and players are asked to give their testimonies. They share how faith in Jesus affects their lives in and out of the spotlight of the game. The first year my husband was invited to share, he said no. He suggested I share our testimonies. Our Baseball Chapel leader wanted my husband to speak. He relented and asked me to stand by his side.

As we stood on the wing of the stage, set up in front of 6,000 or more people, my husband's knees visibly shook. We prayed together and walked on stage. He stumbled over his words at first. I laid my hand on his back and prayed silently. He gathered his thoughts and shared his testimony. The night was a great success as many shared their faith and the crowd roared with, "Amen!" Jesus was glorified.

My husband has spoken at many events now, still not comfortably but God glorifying anyway. God has given him a place to share his love for Jesus and all God has done in his life. Once he released his anxiety to God and made the focus what God wanted him to do, it became easier for him.

Our platform isn't created to be self-centered. A godly platform is kingdom-centered and others-oriented. A kingdom-centered platform builds from a foundation of who God is and why we serve Him. God has chosen us to do special work on earth. Jesus' life, death, and Resurrection was to come to the earth as a human, die on the Cross in the place of each sinner, and to rise from the dead to bring eternal life to each of us. Our lives are to showcase the glory of God.

The realization I was chasing numbers and not representing Christ came with a Scripture passage my husband and I have committed to his job in baseball: "Whatever you do, work at it with all your heart, as working for the Lord, not for human masters" (Colossians 3:23). I had been obeying human masters, those people who told me numbers were important. The work for the Lord, glorifying Him, is what is truly important.

Working for the Lord means centering our lives on His kingdom and living out His amazing love, forgiveness, and mercy. God wants to use us *wherever* we are in life. Whether that's with baby puke on your shoulder and crying kids at your feet, in a cubicle or store, roaming the halls of a hospital, on a baseball field, or with extra time on your hands, God wants you! Get out of His way trying to build a group to follow you. Lead others to follow Him.

Ready to listen and be led, I delved into God's Word to guide me in how God perceives influence. Sincere faith forms a desire to do what is right and true in God's view. We look less to the numbers of who and how we are influencing others. Being sincere in our faith directs our gaze to the relationships we are building on God's foundation. This experience keeps us grounded in the Word of God, creating impactful moments. Every minute God gives us is so we can love and live for the glory of God. We seek to be others-oriented, sharing his love.

Allowing God to work through us comes from a pure heart motivated on who God is, not who we are. We love and serve Him without personal gain based on His power, not our own. I was jealous of the amount of influence my husband had in his job. The jealousy was self-centered. I wanted to have large audiences to hear me talk about the gospel. Me. Me. Me. The desire to have a large number of people to influence was about me and my agenda, not God and His love for me. We have to be a willing vessel.

When I was very young, I was sick a great deal. My aunt said that she never thought I would make it past five years old. As a five-year-old girl, this statement was disconcerting. Was I going to die? As I grew older, many of my family would tell me God had a special plan for me because He "let me live." The thought of a grand plan became an enormous burden. I waited and waited for God to do something big. For many years I felt I was wasting time and failing God.

What was my purpose on this earth? What was my plan for life? I realized once I committed my life to Jesus and became purposeful in living an intentional life, it isn't what I do but how I glorify God in what He does through me. God calls us to glorify Him through each place we exist.

As my husband and I found ourselves on the missions field of Major League Baseball, we knew God was calling us to disciple young men and women. Once our work became focused on God, working for Him, not for man, our influence changed in a mighty way. We began to aggressively pursue Christ in response to His passionate pursuit of us.

With a good conscience, we can use our influence to share the greatness of God. Our inner awareness of the moral quality of our actions keeps our spirit free to pursue God and impact others. We only have to focus on pleasing one person—God. Pleasing God in our actions allows us to pour out His love on others. God is the force of influence. He uses us as His willing vessel. God possesses the power, not us.

As Christians, we are in a fight every day to be successful for Jesus. Every day we fight against our sinful nature and the world's views of success. Remember, the enemy uses every opportunity to attack us and separate us from God. The attacks were confirmed, over and over again, when I began to make changes in my life, letting God's glory shine. The enemy does not want us to be a light and let God's glory shine. He is on the prowl looking for his next victim (1 Peter 5:8).

We have to be alert to fight the good fight at all times. To wage this battle, we need to stay in God's Word and connected to the Holy Spirit. Cleansing our spirit of the distractions that arise, staying close to God and knowing His love in our lives, enables us to represent the love of God to others. Living out the love of God and the love for others is fighting the good fight.

Fighting the good fight of faith is not only fighting to maintain our belief in God and His promises. We are also sustaining our faith to participate in Jesus's victory.

Keeping our faith and living victorious for Jesus is established on the foundation of sincere faith. Genuine faith gives us a foundation to listen to the truth and share it with others. Our faith leads us to do what is right and to glorify God through all we say, do, and are. It allows us to make our life a platform to glorify God. The light shining through our lives is a product of our beliefs and faith in a God who is more amazing than we could ever imagine.

God wants to use each of us in a mighty way. He wants to increase opportunities to share His love, forgiveness, and mercy. By examining the resources in front of us, we can release them to God to use as He wishes.

Being struck by God's glory and greatness exposes what He can accomplish right where we are. Transformation begins with a humble heart, and extended hands release the past hurts, hang-ups, and hardships we have been carrying. Open hands reaching out to others stabilizes our feet on the platform God desires.

Deception happens when we believe we must influence large numbers of people to make a difference for the kingdom. Small is great. I didn't believe this when I was at home with three little boys. Our biggest platform is when we are with those little ones. I struggled with what difference I was making among the dirty diapers and 3 a.m. feedings. And it only seemed to continue as I struggled to keep up with all the activities that carried us through middle and high school.

A fellow homeschool mom profoundly spoke into my life when I voiced my struggles of not feeling as if I was making a difference or doing anything that mattered. She said as moms we are educating the next generation of leaders. Whether we are homeschooling, stay-at-home moms, or working parents, we have a responsibility and a unique platform to nurture our children. We can change the world by preparing them to impact the world.

Jesus was born, lived, and crucified all in a movement to change the world. He came as God in the flesh to show the love, forgiveness, and mercy of our Lord. The gospel builds a kingdom, not just our ability to make a difference. Connecting to one person draws another to Christ. We are to make ourselves available to those among us, who we have contact with daily. We also use the gospel to help followers of Christ grow closer to Jesus.

Linking arms with one another makes Christians stronger. Developing new friendships takes purposeful action. Make a list of people you know. Who have you had contact with today? Can't think of anyone? Sometimes it happens when we are in seasons of not being able to reach out—like when we have little kids, are sick, or work from home. However, we do come in contact with people we might not think of quickly—such as the other mothers we see at the park, the staff at the doctor's office, the person we work with, or the person we talk with on the phone.

We may not have contact each day with many people, but we make contact with others during the week. Put them on your list. Not only do we influence these people but also they affect us. When I was in high school, I surrendered my life to Christ only to walk away during my college years and twenties. During the breakdown of my marriage, I became aware of my need—Jesus. It didn't happen in a mega church or an extensive outreach sponsored by a pastor or organization with a huge platform. It happened when I was sitting with a mom on the baseline of a Little League baseball field in rickety fold-up chairs. While snacking on pretzels that had been touched by a hoard of dirty-handed kids, she asked me my story. She listened.

Then she shared the amazing story of her journey and how Jesus knitted His love, forgiveness, and mercy through it all.

This woman's platform wasn't on a stage in front of thousands or even hundreds. Her platform was her fold-up chair at Tar Park in Brighton, Massachusetts, among yelling children on the playground behind us. The interruptions of one of her six children needing to potty or my three boys "starving to death" stopped the story at times.

And so we sat and shared. My new friend didn't make me feel guilty or regretful. God gave me hope and joy. Those rickety chairs held one woman sharing her story with another woman who was broken and failing to keep it all together. Tar Park was the unique platform God had given us.

I realized I have a very comfortable group of women I include in my life. I can feel safe with my like-minded friends in any circumstance. I have to be purposeful to connect with people outside my comfort group. It has to be a holistic approach, no division of secular and sacred. How am I representing the gospel to the checkout lady at the grocery store? What is the customer service representative on the phone feeling when I become frustrated? Do they see God or anger? How are we representing the gospel? The gospel influences people through us.

When our feet are firmly planted on the gospel, we are the vessel God uses to distribute His Word. Our responsibility is to tell of God's goodness. I had gotten lost in strengthening numbers, not relationships. I am a very relational person. I love to talk with people and hear their stories, but I pushed that aside.

Our stories are what make us who we are. Listening to others' stories opens a dialogue, which builds relationships. I don't ever want to get so far from people that relationships aren't flourishing. God's glory is put on display through these relationships; God has an opportunity to work in and through others.

In John 4, we find the account of the woman at the well. A story many of us have repeatedly heard about Jesus stepping across the secular and sacred line. He was in Samaria, a land of shunned people. These were not His chosen people, yet He was accepted there.

The woman at the well was not a perfect, dutiful woman. She had been married many times and wasn't married to the current man in her life. Her reputation was so blemished that she had to go to the well when no other women were around. Jesus asked her for water. The Samaritan woman pointed out their differences, giving excuses as to why He shouldn't be talking with her. She didn't tell Him her life story, Jesus already knew. He told her many things about her life that only she knew. First, she believed Jesus was a prophet that knew about the Messiah to come. Jesus revealed He was the Messiah. She believed Him.

Leaving her water jar, she went into the town when the disciples returned with food for Jesus. The Samaritan woman told the people what she had experienced. She returned with many people who believed in Him because of what she said. Then they met Jesus face-to-face, and many more believed.

The woman at the well shared with others about her experience with Jesus. She brought people to Him for them to experience Him and His words. The disciples brought food back to Jesus, but no people. Even though they walked daily with Jesus, they were not bringing people back to experience time with Him. They did not talk with people and build relationships, even though they had a larger platform as the chosen twelve. The woman's testimony created more followers because of Jesus, not because of her abilities. God used an ordinary, sinful woman. He uses us the same way. God uses our everyday lives more than we could ever ask or imagine.

In those rickety chairs and many meetings after, my friend guided me into a deeper understanding and belief by leading me to Jesus.

We opened a Bible together to learn more about the Messiah. We met with Him. Jesus led me to a deeper faith.

Through the journey of answering the question of what God is doing through me, I looked to the one who had led people better than any other before or after—Jesus, God in the flesh. Jesus came to do the will of God on earth. He came to save us from ourselves. Jesus came to fulfill a prophecy and to abolish the law. He came to seek the lost and save us from sin. Jesus gave us eternal life by sacrificing His own. He lived to provide us with a pattern of holy living to emulate. Jesus is King, the King of creating a following because of the gospel.

Even still, holding onto past trappings of hurts, hang-ups, and hardships continued to impede my forward momentum. Being the work in progress that I am, I have times when I question. I doubt my worth, my abilities, and my purpose. I release them over and over, then pick them up once again. This process of growing deeper with Christ, allowing His power to work in my spirit, and desiring His work through me, continues to define who I am.

Who are we in Christ? We are fishers of men. Our platform is building relationships to gather more fishers of men. When Jesus called His first disciples, Simon Peter, Andrew, James, and John, He approached them while they were fishing. Jesus told them to drop their nets and follow Him. He told them to come with Him, and He would make them a new type of fishermen. It says they immediately dropped their nets and followed Him. None of them hung onto their nets (Matthew 4:18–22).

We continue to pick up our nets. Letting go of our nets allows us to follow Jesus fully. Progress is when we release them once we realize our hands are full. Showing others God's grace and releasing those nets through our stories nurtures others' faith.

Being fishers of men, representing the gospel through what we say, do, and are builds God's kingdom and glorifies Him. Our platform is our story. Our testimony is the entrance to building relationships with others. Their story creates a deeper connection to Christ and us.

Taking stock of what we are doing within our families begins to build relationships and the stage God has given you. Start at home. Lead your family. Love them with God's love. Forgive and give mercy to those around you. Here we build the foundation for all God is preparing for us. We are educating future leaders.

Many times we want the process of serving God to be beautiful and useful while being painless, quick, and explainable. When God uses us, He uses our past to show others our complete dependence on him. His glory is displayed through us even in our pain. Our uniqueness draws those to us who need to see Jesus the way we did during our trials.

Ask friends to walk the walk with you. Earlier I talked about sharing this journey with a group of friends. Those are the close-knit group where you feel safe and secure. Now reach out to others, people you don't know as well. Ask them to tell you their story. Then listen. Really listen. As your relationship grows, share your grace story—how has God worked in you—and share what He is doing through you to glorify Him. Begin to change the world around you on this growing platform.

Each day we can look for those people God wants to place in our care. Positioning ourselves to receive the appointment where God has placed us, with whom He has placed us, gives us the opportunity to share the gospel and equip others to do the same.

God has given you a platform. Use it! Refuse to think you are the end of the blessing that comes with the platform. Ask God to change and use you for His glory. Love each other with actions and truth, building relationships based on God's glory, allowing the Holy Spirit to lead and guide us, pulling us to the people He wants to bless.

God gives us each a platform—an area where He places us to show His glory. Your platform may be like mine was as a stay-at-home mom, a large platform like my husband's, or somewhere in between.

Our platform is to be used to display all of God's glory that reveals the remarkable work He is doing through us. The challenge to us all is to offer ourselves to God to use as He wishes. *Use me, Lord, where I am in this season of life.*

# Living on Mission

## CHAPTER NINE

My spiritual journey has continued to give me an insight into who Jesus is and who I am in Him. As I embraced my God-created platform, I developed a desire to serve each day. I knew I needed to view my life as a mission for God. I had a desire to serve on the missions field but didn't feel God urging me to pursue what I felt deep in my heart.

As a small child, I thought I wanted to be a nun and work in an orphanage. In my early teens, I knew I wanted to be a nurse, but I still had a powerful feeling I was to do missions work abroad. God had put this on my heart. All my life I felt I was called to work on the missions field.

When I met my husband and we were married, we became busy pursuing our careers—his as a baseball coach and mine as a critical care nurse. I still thought about missions work but knew I wouldn't be able to do the type of work I wanted in that season of life. I put the desire to work on the missions field on the back burner, even though it was still heavy on my heart. Over the years we did work in each of the communities we lived in, through foster care and volunteer work.

I continued to have a strong urging to go to a poor country and help the orphans and widows. When my kids were older, I began to seek out organizations to travel with or groups to tag alongside. Every time I tried to find a place to serve, my attempts failed. God had a different plan. I didn't go to a missions field that was desolate and in despair, as I had envisioned. We found ourselves in a place where people calculate success and influence based on their personal performance and accumulation.

We struggle many times in our lives with God's purpose for us. His guidance is much different from our own sense of purpose in our lives apart from God. In *The Purpose Driven Life*, Rick Warren writes, "It's not about you. The purpose of your life is far greater than your own personal fulfillment, your peace of mind, or even your happiness. It's far greater than your family, your career, or even your wildest dreams and ambitions. . . . You were born by His purpose and for His purpose."

We found our missions field in Major League Baseball. I never dreamed I'd be called to minister to wealthy young men and women who seemed to need nothing. I didn't think these people were desperate for Jesus. They had food and shoes. I wanted hungry, shoeless children to serve.

We are very happy to be part of the baseball family. It took a while to see this was the missions field where God wanted to use us. He wanted to work through us right where we were. I talked myself out of serving over and over because I couldn't see the whole picture.

Our platform to spread the word of God was within the walls of a baseball stadium and our mission among the people there. Our missions field wasn't only the players, coaches, and wives. It was the janitor, the concession worker, the beer vendor, the peanut man, and anyone else we encounter.

Once I evaluated my heart and truly listened to what God wanted me to do for Him, I enjoyed our missions field. The need is there. Over the years I have been pleasantly surprised that people desire to know Jesus in every walk of life. They all need Christ. We all need Christ. It is not what we do, but what He does.

We have been fortunate, in our baseball time, to experience and win a World Series. After we won, I saw one of our players, who had been a large contributor in the playoffs, standing by himself watching the team celebrate. I congratulated him and asked if he was OK. "I am standing here thanking Jesus that I have Him. I have always wanted this," he gestured to the celebration of a World Series win, "but if this was all the hope I had, it would be over in less than an hour. I have Jesus and His hope for eternity." His response sticks with me each year as we serve on the missions field where God has placed us.

We stood quietly for a short while; then the player added, "I am sad for all these guys who have reached the peak of their lives. This is what they will always try to live up to every day. They will always grasp this feeling to size up happiness and success." I knew what he would say next. He, his wife, my husband, and I had all committed our lives to Christ within the year before the World Series win. The focus of what mattered had changed. Peace came from Jesus. We now calculated success by glorifying God in what we did, said, and were.

"I am thankful that I am content with wherever God takes me, asks me to do, and blesses me with after this win." The player was happy for the win, but he knew tomorrow he wouldn't be searching for this experience to fulfill him again. He was content with wherever or whatever God brought his way. "But godliness with contentment is great gain. For we brought nothing into the world, and we can take nothing out of it" (1 Timothy 6:6–7).

I work in the missions field Jesus has given me, remembering the player's comment, "I have Jesus and His hope for eternity." No matter the wins or losses, the success or injuries, the fame or money, I want each person to know the hope of Jesus. I have accepted the missions work God has given me to display His glory in the place we live.

Many years ago I heard a sermon that talked about our responsibility to live each day in response to the sacrifice Jesus made and the love He has for us. Living on mission is living our lives focused on the work God desires to do through us to bring Him glory.

"Jesus, what do You want me to do for You today?" is a sticky note I still have in the front of my Bible, a reminder of Jesus' desire to guide and my commitment to obey. Many times I find myself sitting and waiting to see what God will do without taking the first step in faith. We have to take a step in faith to see what He can accomplish through us. Living on mission is taking purposeful steps in faith, allowing the Lord to work through us according to His power.

Pastor Francis Chan and his wife made a decision to serve in East Africa for their twentieth wedding anniversary. They had been researching vacation trips to Fiji and other exotic places. In a video they posted, Chan detailed the process by which they decided to instead serve in an underdeveloped country. He realized that their most impactful encounters together as a couple had been when they served others. Their story is evidence of a missional life.

Waking up each day and asking the Lord, "What do You want me to do for You today?" is the first step in faith to see what God will do through you. It is the first step in living on mission. Step out in faith and move where God leads.

God has a plan for our lives. "'For I know the plans I have for you,' declares the LORD, 'plans to prosper you and not to harm you, plans to give you hope and a future'" (Jeremiah 29:11). If you read my writings, you will see me refer to this often. It has been confirmed over and over again in my life. When we surrender to Christ, knowing He has our backs, we are aware we can fulfill what He has called us to do, with His guidance.

"One day you will be at the place you always wanted to be." This quote broke my heart when I read it on a friend's Facebook profile. I lived in that place once before. I lived in a place where maybe tomorrow will be the day, a specific car would make me happy, a bigger house would make the perfect home for our family, the perfect job would fulfill us. And while the car was bought, the bigger house was obtained, and the job was offered, *the* day never came. Because none of those things provided perfection, fulfillment, or happiness.

Each day may not be the day you want it to be, but you are given an opportunity every day. No matter what we gain in this lifetime, if we do not have holy contentment in the simple things, we will never have fulfillment or happiness. Let today be the day you find yourself in the place you always wanted to be—in the presence of the Lord and His blessings.

 *There, in the presence of the LORD your God, you and your families shall eat and shall rejoice in everything you have put your hand to, because the LORD your God has blessed you.*

*—Deuteronomy 12:7*

Living on mission is living each day serving others out of the abundance of our faith. During this spiritual trek, I have become more aware of the responsibility God has given me. I became mindful of God's guidance and stepped out in faith to act upon His desires. He asked me to shore up my faith and stand firm. God hid me under the shadow of His wings, protecting me while I moved forward (Ruth 2:12; Psalm 17:8).

Even though we make mistakes and sometimes misunderstand, we shouldn't doubt our worth. We are children of God. He loves and treasures us as His children. God is strong when we are weak and faithful when fear overpowers us. His grace is sufficient when we fall short. His light guides our path as we walk out our faith. Wisely walking with Jesus governs our spiritual travel of serving Him.

How do we live on mission? We have to seek to obey what God has already revealed. Spiritual attacks will come. Stand strong on His Word. Nothing that is contrary to the Word of God can be a godly direction.

Biblical discernment must be a discipline for each and every decision we make. If it does not line up biblically, it is the wrong direction.

We know about distractions and how they make us wander outside of God's will. The Lord knows we will go astray. We need to make it a habit to look to Him often, in prayer, in His Word, and in godly, like-minded friends. It redirects our view from things that are contrary to His direction.

Continue to take the power washer to your spirit, cleaning out all the crevices of junk that builds up in your soul. Keep an open link of communication with Christ through prayer. Our souls are a willing vessel as the Holy Spirit roams freely, giving us direction of His plan.

Living with the intention of an aim or purpose concerning God's calling makes our lives matter. It provides us with intentional and fulfilling direction. I watched a video recently of my son's friend who was in a car accident when he was 15. The accident left him paralyzed from the waist down. The video was of him walking. Yes, walking. He has been blessed to be one of a small number of people with paraplegia to receive a device that helps them stand and walk. The tears flowed as I watched this young man take steps, an answer to many prayers.

He and his family are the prime examples of living on mission. They had a tragic incident happen in their lives, but they didn't let it stop them. They took a time of pause and mourning, then moved forward in faith. God was going to take them to a place of victory. They have spent many days during this experience knowing their friends and family were praying for them. I know there were days, sometimes weeks, of struggles, but they were shining brightly as he took his first steps.

Through all of their battles, they have been a tremendous support system to others. They have linked arms and strengthened others in their times of need. The community has come out in full force to help this young man. We all have different circumstances in our lives where we can encourage and serve others.

Through this continual spiritual journey, my love for God has deepened. It has led to being more confident of God's Word and developed a conviction in my spirit. God's word is infallible. We can be confident His guidance throughout the Bible is valid today. Because of His Resurrection, He is alive in our lives today. His guidance reveals our purpose and meaning in this current day.

Standing alongside godly friends has propelled my faith in God to a place of obedience and accountability. Seeking the wisdom of friends can help determine if our feelings of God's desires are valid. Living with others who are fulfilling God's assignments validates His authority.

When we are determining our daily mission, and those larger ones of the future, assessing our gifts and talents can lead us to God's plans. He doesn't ask us to do work for Him in a way we were not created to do. If He has not wired us in a particular way, those things will not be fulfilled through us.

My boys sang in high school. The older two were part of an *a cappella* group and even had solos. They sang with the teen worship band at times and had a real gift of carrying a tune. Our youngest also sang in musicals on stage, singing a few solos.

Let's just say, God did not give me the gift of singing on key. I can't sing for the life of me. I have a desire but no talent. I know the ability skipped a generation because my husband has the same lack of skill. We are not called to sing on the worship team. No matter how much we desire to serve, we would not torture the congregation with our inabilities.

We each have unique talents and gifts that create our platform and our mission, our calling. Being able to define those skills and abilities is a way to develop an understanding of the work God desires for you to implement. If you don't know what your gifts may be, ask some friends. Ask friends to give you three words they think best describe you. It will help you see your natural gifts.

Being aware of opportunities God presents helps determine our daily mission. Remember my desire to serve overseas? No matter how many organizations I run after or push my way into, I have never been able to schedule a trip. Family commitments, scheduling conflicts, money issues, and all sorts of things come in the way of my being able to fulfill my desire.

During my marriage and mommy duties, I begged the Lord to provide a way for me to serve overseas. I had a stirring in my spirit. I was called to serve at home. My response to God, "I serve at home every day. What do you mean, 'serve at home'?" Air quotation marks and all, I mocked God by asking what He meant. Doors continued to close, and I served at home with my boys, my husband, foster kids, with baseball wives, and with other organizations that do great things in our community. I still yearned to serve abroad. I told you I am a slow learner. And I make God laugh a lot.

During this journey of seeking the immeasurably more God desires to do through me, it became very apparent the direction God did *not* want me to go. I don't know why and don't know if no is a forever answer, but I know He has not provided the opportunity for me yet.

I also began to pray about my desire to serve. God reveals things in the timeliest way. When I prayed, I did so for quite a few days. I want to make an impact for God's kingdom. Then someone tagged me on social media. She tagged a quote I used when I spoke at a Baseball Chapel women's event the year before. She thanked me for discussing how God had created us for unique service. He has not called anyone else to do what He has called us to do in the same exact way. God had created us as unique individuals to do His work. She said she was doing His special work, living on mission.

In her thank-you, God spoke into my spirit. I am making an impact. I am allowing God to use me as He has uniquely given me abilities to serve Him, in the opportunities He places before me, to glorify Him. When I get out of His way and allow Him to use me, His desires become my desires. I fought my call to write for years.

When I finally accepted it, surrendered, and began to write with purpose, the blessings flowed. Of course there were bumps and bruises, headaches and head banging. It was not a straight path to success. Little by little my confidence grew because I was obeying God and understanding His desire to be glorified through the words He gave me.

We can get in God's way trying to figure it all out. Making lists. Tackling tasks. Striving to succeed. We can lose sight of His guidance by looking too far ahead.

All we need to do is to take a step. If we faithfully put one foot in front of the other, He will direct our steps. When the light illuminates the entire plan, it is wonderful; we don't have to question so much. Walking forward, even when the plan is not all laid out, when only one step is illuminated, is faith. Trust in God's providence and love leads us into the calling that is unique to us.

Start where you are. Take one act. Serving others will draw you to where God desires you to serve more. It isn't some magical formula to follow but a relationship to nurture. A relationship of love and understanding creates a desire to help Him and others.

When we find our purpose in life—serving God—we use the resources He has given us to find direction to step out in faith. Our mission is tied to Jesus' mission, "Again Jesus said, 'Peace be with you! As the Father has sent me, I am sending you'" (John 20:21). Jesus commanded us to go and do as He has done in His power and peace.

Each of us is a missionary being called by God to serve others. Serving others where we work, live, and play. Moving from observing to serving. Living with purpose and intent.

Serving others creates value. It creates value in us and the value of Jesus living in and through us. In Mark 2, we read a familiar story— the story of Jesus healing a paralyzed man. Jesus had returned to Capernaum, and many had gathered to see Him. A large crowd gathered inside and outside the house. A group of men had brought their paralyzed friend to see Jesus.

We don't know for sure, but the way these men carried their friend must have been awkward and cumbersome. They may have had a distance to go. In their great faith, they did it.

The men dug a hole in the roof of the house and lowered their friend. I imagine there was dust and chunks of roof falling into the room where Jesus preached. It couldn't have been easy, quiet, or clean.

These men went above and beyond their duty as friends. They carried a heavy man and destructed a man's house without thought of what others might think or say. "When Jesus saw their faith, he said to the paralyzed man, 'Son, your sins are forgiven'" (Mark 2:5).

There were others in the room who were not strong in their beliefs of Jesus' authority. In their thoughts, they questioned His words.

*Immediately Jesus knew in his spirit that this was what they were thinking in their hearts, and he said to them, "Why are you thinking these things? Which is easier: to say to this paralyzed man, 'Your sins are forgiven,' or to say, 'Get up, take your mat and walk'? But I want you to know that the Son of Man has authority on earth to forgive sins." So he said to the man, "I tell you, get up, take your mat and go home." He got up, took his mat and walked out in full view of them all. This amazed everyone and they praised God, saying, "We have never seen anything like this!"*

—vv. 8–12

The paralyzed man was healed because of the faith and commitment of his friends. What if the friends had decided it was too much work to take the man the distance needed to meet Jesus? What if they had given up on their journey because the man was too heavy? What if they stopped because their way through the crowd was too difficult to make? What if they stopped because it wasn't the way it should happen? The healing would not have occurred. The paralyzed man wouldn't have known Jesus.

Challenges, twists, and turns occur when trying to bridge the gap for others. Letting our love of Jesus and His love for us drive us to move from observing to serving helps others find the God of love. The men who took the paralytic to Jesus made a way because of their belief in the power of Jesus and the love of their friend.

My husband and I chose to help a classroom in a local school where we live during the baseball season by providing school supplies for the kids. We only live in this neighborhood during the baseball season, but we know God put us there for a purpose. God provided an opportunity when we opened our eyes and hearts to the surrounding community. We knew we were able to give supplies to one classroom. God had bigger plans.

When talking with the other team wives, they too saw the need and wanted to get involved. Then the team my husband works for heard what we were doing. The community service department of the team added to the supplies. Each year our team honors the memory of Roberto Clemente. Roberto played 18 years in Major League Baseball for the Pittsburgh Pirates. He was actively involved in charity work in Latin America and Caribbean countries throughout his career. He delivered baseball equipment and food to those in need. In 1972, Roberto was killed in a plane crash while en route to Nicaragua. He was delivering aid to victims of a devastating earthquake. On Roberto Clemente Day, the Clemente family, along with players, coaches, wives, and employees, deliver backpacks of school supplies to the neighborhood school. We went from observing to serving. Anyone can do one small deed. God turns our little into His big.

God has placed us in a workplace where we can serve. Not only did we help the students and teachers of the school, but it also connected two busloads of people to a school full of children, teachers, and staff. Looking for opportunities to be a blessing in our workplace reveals connections. When we choose to serve others, God's glory is revealed.

For my family, where we play is a baseball field. I socialize and make deeper connections there. Being present in these places gives us the opportunity to share God's love and sacrifice for our lives. Look around where you spend your social time. There will be chances to serve when you pray and seek God's guidance. It takes crossing the secular and sacred lines and reaching out to those who need a deeper connection with Christ.

There are seasons of our lives when serving is contained in the walls of our home with our children, maybe only being able to reach out to the community once a year. Serving can present itself in many different fashions, but it is always glorifying to God.

Committing to the special work in the season where we live now reveals the work of God in and through us. Never give up, and don't let failure and expectations disappoint you. Get involved in the exchange where you live, work, and play. Choose to view your everyday life as a missionary. I am a missionary, and my mission comes from God. I am not here just to take up space. I am here to share what God has done in me and show what God is doing through me.

At a point in my journey, the pendulum swung from focusing on me to focusing on others. The change came at the perfect time in my life. It wasn't because I had checked off the list of to-dos and miraculously hit a point so that when the bell rang, I embarked on service. It was a God-appointed time to act in faith.

The Holy Spirit changed me from the inside out. At the precise moment, God chose to pull me into the place He desired to do more through me, to do my special work for Him. The Holy Spirit created and orchestrated this perfect timing.

The difference in the works of my to-do list and God's timing is I didn't have to push my way into any service or feel a duty to obey. God provided an empowered, specified time for me to step out in faith and follow His direction to serve. The moment cannot be accurately defined, but as we live it in obedience and follow where God is pulling, we can look back and see His involvement. The time He chooses allows doors to fly open—fear shifts to function, chaos turns to calm, and hope and faith combine to create purpose.

In these moments, when we are not even aware of what is occurring, the Holy Spirit hovers, waiting for us to allow God to work through us. At times we can miss this possibility. The clutter in our spirits and distractions of our busy lives can take us away from the movement of the Holy Spirit. Spiritual attacks can make us cower in fear and miss the signs. Busyness is an absolute blinder to what God desires.

In the Book of Ruth, we see a woman who steps out in faith and loyalty, which ultimately allows her life to form the lineage of Christ's heritage. Ruth was a Moabite who married a man from Bethlehem in Judah after his father had died (Ruth 1:4). Her husband and his brother, father, and mother had come to Moab to live during a time when no king was in place and famine impacted the land.

Naomi, Ruth's mother-in-law, was left with her two sons after her husband's death. They then married two Moabites, one being Ruth. Ten years later, Naomi's two sons also died. Naomi's life was empty now that all of her relatives had died. She heard Bethlehem had food, so she planned to return home. She told both of her sons' wives they were free to go back to their families. There were no other male family members for them to marry, which was customary at that time.

One left to return to her family, but Ruth stayed by Naomi's side. She committed to remain with Naomi. Ruth was loyal and selfless in her devotion to remain by Naomi's side despite unexpected circumstances. She fully committed to Naomi with no prospect for her except to share in Naomi's devastation. Ruth declared to follow Naomi's God, and if she were ever to leave Naomi, the Lord would deal with her severely.

When she and Ruth returned to Bethlehem, the women who saw Naomi asked, "Can this be Naomi?" Naomi told them to call her Mara, which means "bitter." Her explanation for the name divulges her sense of desolation. Ruth stayed by her side even as a foreigner in a new land.

Ruth took a step of faith to follow her mother-in-law to a land where she would be a stranger. When the circumstance looked as if there was inevitable hurt, she trusted in the love of God. Naomi was empty, not knowing the fullness of God standing beside her.

God is always plotting for us. He puts people beside us to help guide us. Or He places us next to the people He needs us to link arms and join with. The story at the beginning of Ruth looked like a tragedy but it is one that turns into beauty and joy, trusting in the love of God.

Hurting people surround us. It may not be apparent, but everyone has a story to tell. We need to listen. When we don't know what to do, we must step out in faith. Ruth stepped out in faith and showed up in Boaz's field. It was no coincidence she was there. The timing was in God's appointed time. Ruth only went to the field to pick up what was left behind, enough to feed herself and Naomi. She was not on the hunt for a husband, yet the Lord directed her to the appropriate field.

Our plans and God's plan for us are not exclusive of one another. He knows what it will take to fulfill His plan for us and pulls us in that direction. Even when we take a detour, He is more than able to redirect our steps to align with His. The insignificant moments in our lives are often the ones He uses for significant direction toward His goal. And if God closes a door, no strength in us could open it if He doesn't intend us to go through it.

When Boaz arrived in his field, he noticed Ruth. He showed her favor and allowed her to glean in the field. Boaz told his workers to lay more wheat where she worked so she could gather more grain. When she arrived home, Naomi was astonished at the favor shown to Ruth. Naomi had hope for her future, food, and a family. Boaz was a kinsman-redeemer, one who could restore Naomi's family. She was right in having hope. Boaz married Ruth; he was indeed their redeemer. God can use anyone who is available to Him.

Boaz and Ruth had a son named Obed. Here is where the story gets even better. Obed was the father of Jesse and Jesse the father of David. Where does the genealogy take us? Directly to the birth of Jesus. In Matthew 1, we see the genealogy of Jesus. Ruth is named as a foremother of Jesus, setting the stage for the ultimate Redeemer.

The lineage of Jesus was helped along by the faith and loyalty of one woman. She placed her trust in the Lord and took a step in faith. God fulfilled His ultimate plan by putting her in the right place at the right time. When God puts you somewhere, it is no coincidence. No failures occur when we obey and live on mission. When we step out in faith, God shows up. We can use our time to mentor other believers, linking arms with them, because telling others about the great love and sacrifice of Christ glorifies God.

It is God's nature to reveal Himself. You must be willing to obey even when you do not know the plan. We are not naturally inclined to step out and share our faith or link arms with another person. Living life and accomplishing our tasks is much easier than taking a chance of living on mission. We must do it even though we may not want to.

Spend time with Jesus. Read His Word. Pray. Let Him pull us in the direction He intends. If we don't feel confident in where we should go, we have to walk forward until He directs us to move a different way.

Step out in faith, believing God will lead, guide, and direct you. Look for others around you and listen to their stories. Encourage them while presenting God's love through yourself.

Be still and listen while doing the hard stuff. We can achieve stillness in our spirit even when our lives are busy. Find the stillness to connect with Him. We have been uniquely created to do a special work for the Lord. Let's take the first step—belief and trust in the one who makes all things possible. We are blessed by God to be a blessing to others. Let's not miss out on a chance to make a difference. Live each day looking for those unexplainable moments when God reveals a plan. Trust God in His direction by living out His mission, sharing Him.

We each work in the missions field Jesus has given us. And we live each day with the certainty we have Jesus and His hope for eternity. God wants everyone to build a relationship with Him and know the hope of Jesus. Build relationships. Encourage one another. Share the gospel. Live a life that matters to God.

CONCLUSION

Discovering the Opportunities We Have When the Lord Is Freely Moving in and through Us

# Well Done!

## CHAPTER TEN

This journey has taught me many things, but the one I continue to carry most tightly is that I am living my life according to His power, not my own. When I shared the story of this entire adventure with one of my sons, he asked how it has changed me and if it had changed my beliefs. I sat deep in thought because I didn't think the foundation of my belief was different, but I was definitely clinging to it with more conviction. I want my life to leave a legacy of what I believe.

Our conversation turned to an obituary I had recently read online. It was a hilarious account of the man's life and his legacy. The discussion took a sharp turn when my son asked what I wanted my obituary to read. He intently listened as I said; "She slid headfirst into heaven with dust flying around her." I meant it. He suggested that since I was a writer, I needed to pen it, and he would read the missive aloud.

I want to live life healthy, robust, dynamic, lively, active, spirited, and to the fullest. When I get to heaven, I want to see Jesus smile ear-to-ear as the dust settles after my slide. I want Him to say to me, "Well done, my good and faithful servant."

I have been a spiritual traveler through this transformational process. As I began traversing the process of resolving the answer to the question my pastor asked, I couldn't comprehend what an adventure it would be. The route was not straight and narrow with well-lit pathways, answers revealed at every stage, and the meaning of my life written on stone tablets. The expedition including digging and uprooting, flying and crashing, smiling and crying while not getting complete answers but a deeper connection with my Savior.

At some points, when the enemy ambushed my spirit, I didn't know if I could go on. God reminded me that when we are at our weakest, He is most powerful. His power pulled me through. I didn't like unearthing the ugly hidden hurts, hang-ups, and hardships. They wanted to drag me down into darkness and self-pity. The enemy didn't want me to see any of God's goodness through it, but I could not let that happen. I wanted to know the answer to the question in my life, "What is God doing in and through you?" In my journey I also began to ask myself, "What do you want your meeting with Jesus to be like when you meet Him face-to-face?"

Can you envision that meeting? What will it be like to stand in His presence? At first, the thought of seeing Him in all His glory brought peace to my soul. Then a question popped into my head that sent a shiver down my spine, "When I stand face-to-face with Jesus, what will He say to me?"

Will God ask me questions? Will I have answers? Will He ask why I didn't serve others? Will He ask why I chose one path when He clearly lit the other? Will He be happy with decisions I made? Will He wrap me in His arms and shout, "Welcome home, my good and faithful servant!" What will my life look like through His eyes? Will I find myself speechless for the first time in my life?

During my spiritual travel exploring God's desires, I revisited these questions. What will Jesus say? What would He say as I am today? It propelled me to seek the desires of God even more intently. Our lives need to be crafted to fulfill Jesus' desires in and through us, so when we are directly in front of Jesus, He will exclaim, "Well done, my good and faithful servant."

The more I bore and dredged into my soul, the greater healing God offered. As I healed, the passion for knowing more urged me on. I wanted more of God. The closer I came to Jesus the more the need to deepen my understanding of His will surged. Understanding led to intensified concentration on His guidance in my life. I couldn't contain the excitement of my spiritual transformation. I had to tell others and allow the love of Christ in me to begin to work through me.

Was this new knowledge I gained through this process? No, but it was fresh and unearthing, the birthing of a clearer and a deeper connection to Christ. As I traveled the many miles of spiritual transformation, taking me from a complacent and stagnant faith to one of remarkable living, the goal of my life came in question. What was the goal of my life? I get caught up in the things I am learning and doing and forget the real meaning of life—glorifying God.

Why do we glorify God? Do we glorify Him to be a good Christian? What is the ultimate goal?

*His master replied, "Well done, good and faithful servant! You have been faithful with a few things; I will put you in charge of many things. Come and share your master's happiness!"*
*—Matthew 25:21*

If our goal is to hear this response when we see Jesus, we must craft our lives to fulfill that purpose. Our faith is the pathway to fulfillment. After reviewing all of the experiences, I had to wonder what was holding me back from living a life well done, a remarkable life.

In John 6, we read the familiar story of Jesus feeding a great crowd of people. Jesus had crossed over the Sea of Galilee to the far shore. Many people were on their way to Jerusalem for Passover. They followed Jesus because of the miracles and healing they had seen Him perform.

Jesus went up onto the mountainside and sat with His disciples. He saw the crowd coming toward Him. Do we see the few or the crowd before us? Do we see who the Lord is calling us to serve? Do we see the life He wants us to live? Jesus saw the crowd. He had compassion for their physical and spiritual needs. Jesus tested the disciples' faith with questions. He wants to test our faith also.

Jesus asked Philip where they were to buy bread for the people to eat. Jesus asked in order to stretch Philip's faith. He wants to stretch our faith also. Philip thought logically and knew it was costly, more than eight months' wages, to buy enough food to feed the number of people present. A boy near them had five loaves of bread and two fish. The disciples didn't think the bread and fish were enough to feed the crowd. We often think what we can offer is not sufficient either.

Jesus asked everyone to sit, He gave thanks, and they served the food. They had as much as they wanted. What difference would it make if I gave what God asks of me? All of me to Him. Jesus always multiplies the sacrifices. When the disciples gathered the leftovers, there were twelve baskets filled with pieces of the bread. One for each disciple. Enough and more.

Little did the boy know the lunch his mother packed would have such a significant impact. Jesus challenges the motives of His followers. We often look to Him for what He can give us, as if following Jesus results in a Christian spin on the American dream. Rather we should see what He has given to us and what we can give back. Believe in Him who God has sent and place all our trust and hope in Him. It calls for total surrender.

When we wake up feeling defeated, we can realize joy and victory are not in our power. Only through His strength are all things possible, His power to do abundantly more in and through us (Ephesians 3:20). Always be reminded of His great love for us.

To craft a well-done life we need to see the crowd. Each day it is an active battle. We proactively engage in these fights through the Word of God and the power of the Holy Spirit against our sinful nature, the world's values, and the devil's schemes. We win battles when we are in the Word and full of the Holy Spirit. We fight because we have experienced God's love and are representing the love of God to others. As children of God, we have been charged to engage in war against the enemy. As we grow in knowledge, the grip on our faith becomes firm. Continue to learn. We cannot hold onto our faith if we are not growing in our knowledge of the Bible. We show others passion for the Lord. Passion grows with understanding.

Many people think we should let our conscience be our guide. *No!* Let God be our guide. By increasing our knowledge and understanding of Scripture, God will increase our practice of faith. We have to apply it to our life.

During this spiritual transformation, I saw a friend who had lost a lot of weight and looked joyous and healthy. She had been on a great workout program and was seeing excellent results. I bought the program but decided before I did the workout that I would watch the DVD to see how hard it was. I sat on the couch and watched the workouts before trying a few. I continued to eat what I wanted. I saw no great results, unlike my friend. I know . . . I am a work in progress. Not until I took the workouts seriously and ate the amount of food the program instructed did I see positive results. The more I followed the plan, the more results I saw.

If we sit on the couch and watch the DVDs but never do the exercise, we only accumulate the knowledge. There will never be any change, just knowledge. Change occurs when we apply knowledge to our lives. Our spiritual lives, the deeper connection to Christ, and the transformation in our lives doesn't happen by taking in only the lessons. Take the knowledge of this spiritual journey and apply it to life. Be transformed.

Transformation happens when we defeat the negative response to the enemy's attempts and cling to Jesus. The enemy wants to wreck our lives and leave us stranded without hope. He tries to destroy us. He doesn't want to see positive change. Our strength will not propel us in the battle with the enemy. Only God's power can defeat him. Rebelling and trying to do it on our program may tempt us to see ourselves as God. God wants us to stick to our faith in Him to overcome the enemy.

There is strength in numbers. Surround yourself with people who will hold your arm up when you get tired. When circled by friends filled with faith, hope, and joy, we find God's strength in those who help support us. Don't go at this alone. Live life to the fullest with others. At times we must go up the mountain and be alone with God, and then on other occasions, we need friends to help hold us up.

Seize the moments God gives us. Strive to keep a close watch on how we are living out our faith. We see what we believe in how we are living out our faith. Pay attention to what you say and do. Our actions show what we believe. Our behavior doesn't change God. God changes our behavior according to His power through grace and mercy.

Our response reveals what we believe about God. Seek to be an example of godly character. We must devote our lives to glorifying God. Steward your lives and gifts faithfully. Put fear behind you and use your God-given gifts to glorify Him. Be obedient and leave the results to Him. Randy Alcorn says in his book *Eternal Perspectives*, "What you do with your resources in this life is your autobiography."

Stories are formed over our lifetime. Our stories create our legacy to those we know and love. If my obituary is going to reflect a life lived to the fullest, I must submit each day to Jesus. I pray that everything I do, say, and am reflects His light in my life.

I questioned my life story and thought about how that face-to-face meeting with Jesus would look. I began to note the actions and thoughts I wanted Jesus to be proud of in my life. I analyzed the gifts God has given me, even the gift of gab, and determined some actions I could take to glorify Him more in my daily living. I wanted to learn more about the Bible. I gathered a few friends, and we went straight to Scripture. Many of the women didn't want to share out loud, so I talked and encouraged. I held their arms until they were ready to share. It was rewarding to learn with one another, glorifying God where we were—in a park with kids running wild.

When crafting our lives to be a life well done, we have to use our gifts to glorify Him. When we have experienced the free gift of grace Jesus offers, we cannot hold back love for others. God's love for us compels us to care for others. We have to be cautious to not act out of selfish intent, to be patted on the back, or gain notoriety. We love others with humility and encouragement. We seek out the vulnerable and help them—meeting their needs instead of our own. When we do what He is calling us to do we are not neglecting the gifts He has given us. Put fear behind. Step out in faith.

When we serve others without the selfish intent of looking like a good person, the light of Jesus shines. The fight diminishes when our selfish desires are less important than our love for God. Temptations to look at our selfish desires are oh-so-desirable. Becoming selfless, loving God more than others, and others more than ourselves is the goal. The race we run is one of eternal value, the value of Jesus' sacrifice. We must allow Jesus to lead us daily. We cannot run from suffering but we can embrace it, relying on the strength given to us through the Holy Spirit. We have to put our plans and desires aside, turn our lives over to Him, and obey Him. We must commit our whole lives to Him.

This travel through the deep crevices of my spiritual being has been adventurous and challenging. We often think we have reached the pinnacle in our spiritual lives when we [fill in the blank]. When I reach the faith peak. When I overcome a particular habit, hardship, or hang-up. When I have a miraculous God moment. When God is glorified through me.

Then comes spiritual attack, overwhelming distractions, or an over-crowded schedule. Spiritually we live on a roller coaster of moments. We are never there until we are face-to-face with Jesus.

To live the immeasurably more God wants to do through us, we have to accept abundant living is not in our power but through His. His power working through us is more than words. It is profound obedience, fighting for justice for those who cannot fight for themselves, advocating for someone who cannot advocate for themselves, and teaching by example, not telling. Sacrifice is crucial.

Our lives become profoundly obedient in the calling God has for us. Sacrificing words for the action required to live a well-done life begins with self-control and discipline. God-centered thoughts develop control and obedience.

Prayer connects us daily with God, centering our thoughts on His power working within us. When we talk to Jesus, He hears us. A powerful prayer life keeps our connection secure. Prayer is not a means to an end but a foundation to lay our lives on.

A powerful prayer life strengthens our connection with Christ. As you pray, seeking the Lord and an understanding of His will for your life, do not lose your focus on Him. When you do get an answer or direction, it is easy to focus on the unknown. Don't become consumed in finding the answer. Become consumed with Him and His power working in and through you.

Our intent should be to get alone with God. It may not be physically possible, but we can make it spiritually possible. Prayer with self-controlled, kingdom-centered thoughts keeps us in a deeper connection with Him, even amidst the chaos of life. Selfishness lacks humility. Humility, in our lives, focuses our thoughts.

We may pray to ask God to move in our lives, save us from our hardships, or give us something. When God provides us with the answer, we may become consumed with the fulfillment and lose focus on Him. When He doesn't respond the way we think He should, we lose our focus on Him. We become absorbed with the unfairness and walk alone through the suffering. We are not alone, ever. Go up that mountain and get alone with Jesus.

John the Baptist was a great example of getting away and drawing closer to God. He was the son of Zechariah and Elizabeth, Mary's cousin. Elizabeth became pregnant at an old age and Gabriel, the angel, came to Zechariah and told him John, his son, would go before Jesus to make ready the people for the coming of the Lord (Luke 1:13–17). John was born and lived to fulfill Isaiah's prophecy of being the one who would announce the coming Messiah (3:16).

John went into the wilderness until the time of his public ministry. He began his ministry along the Jordan River preaching the message of repentance, announcing the coming of the Messiah, and preparing the way for the Lord. John practiced fasting and taught others to pray. He was extremely influential among the people.

John prepared himself by going away in the wilderness. His life was to glorify God in all that he said, did, and was. John knew man could only receive what was given from heaven. "He must become greater; I must become less" (John 3:30).

Decreasing our own wants, needs, and desires to fulfill God's purpose for us accomplishes a life well lived. Every day we fight against our sinful nature and the world's views. The enemy uses every opportunity to attack us and separate us from God. Every time I begin to make changes in my life, when God's glory starts to shine through me, I come under attack one way or another. This only confirms that I am in God's will because the enemy does not want me to be a light and let God's glory shine.

We have to be alert to fight the good fight at all times. We must focus on God's Word and stay connected to the Holy Spirit if we are to engage in the battle effectively. We can represent God to others by staying close to God and knowing His love in our lives. Glorifying God's love within us conveys His love to those around us.

There will be struggles. Life is not stepping up a ladder one rung at a time, leaving the lessons and circumstances behind and finding glory here on earth. Growth is a roller coaster ride of ups and downs. We search for the next answer to a lesson God needs to teach us, while reaching out to others, joining together, and being pulled in the direction He wants us to go.

In living a life well done versus well said, we must continue to seek His face. Each day we come up against circumstances that send us into a spiral of self-centered thinking. It doesn't matter how we feel in those moments; it matters how we respond. We have to keep our mind on Him and our eyes on the word. Our hearts trust His guidance, and our souls can feel the total peace that comes with His Spirit.

Our minds play games on us. A war of words and thoughts rage in our heads, keeping us confused when we are not soaked in Scripture. Seeking God's wisdom and guidance, reading His Word, and praying for the discernment to our emotions against His Word results in a Christlike action. Our actions, in response to God's sacrifice and His Word, put God's glory on display.

Seeing the need of others, sacrificing our self-focused mind-set, and stepping out in faith guides us to live on mission with the goal of a life well done. Look beyond what you see and depend on His Holy Spirit. Be at the ready to be used by Him.

A job well done doesn't add another to-do list of things we have to accomplish. It is a lifestyle. When we believe in the sacrifice Jesus made on the Cross for us and allow Him to live in us actively, we are pleasing to God. Thinking of it as a to-do list steals our joy. We don't have to keep a list of rules and regulations but a deep connection with Him.

Don't miss out on the abundant life God desires by not taking risks to live life to the fullest according to His power. Living a well-done life, with the goal of winning the prize at the end of the race, takes risk. The risk happens when we think and act differently from the people around us. If we are focused on pleasing people, we have taken our gaze off the prize. Abundant life is accomplished when we are actively storing our treasures in heaven, not gathering more stuff in our lives.

Life mirrors a long race with checkpoints along the way. Hurts and hardships will try to take us off the path Jesus has lit for us to follow. Pause. Be still with Him. Then live life finishing the course, preparing to meet Jesus face-to-face.

Connecting to Jesus is more important than any experience on this earth when you are living life well done. Can we imagine what being near Him will be like—standing before Him with our arms wide open?

Seize the moments God has in our lives and, when we are with Him, it will all be worth it! Refuse to believe we are the ends of the blessings that God freely gives—spread the love. The love of God increases the more you share it. Our lives are a lifelong learning process with Christ. We learn, turn to others, and teach from the overpouring love of Christ. Invest in the lives of others by sharing the gospel, living an intentional life with the unique platform God has given us in the missions field he has placed us.

As servants of Christ, we have been entrusted with the revealed knowledge of God. He trusts us as His children to share His message and love. We will be judged by others and criticized by some. In 1 Corinthians 4:1–5, Paul vindicates himself from a group of church leaders who had become influential and self-important. These very believers were Paul's converts. While Paul had gone to spread the gospel, the leaders had become cavalier, prideful, and bossy trying to take over the church. Paul told them he didn't look to them for validation nor did he judge himself. He only looked to the Lord. Paul said the Lord would expose darkness and the motives of man and each would receive their praise from God.

We are tempted to look to others to see what they expect. We look to ourselves for validation, trying to live up to the standards of the world. Living up to the expectations of others leads to emptiness and despair. Our goal is an unwavering sense of worth and an unshakable sense of identity. For this, we look to Jesus. With a goal of well done, we focus on Jesus.

We are not accountable for what gifts God has given others but what He has given us. We have to be faithful with the gifts He gives us. Steward what God gives us in our lives. Others may think that you are better than them in certain situations when God's gifts are used to abundance. Don't be prideful if your gifts are appreciated. Be faithful with what He has given. Accept the gift, and use it to the fullest of God's abilities.

As I walked this expedition of spiritual transformation, I talked with friends about a time they felt an infusion of God's gifts and abilities. I asked how they felt about that, and the similarities were astounding. A baseball couple at a Christian conference discussed how sometimes they feel guilty for where God has placed them. They were in their midtwenties, and their income was sizable. His endorsements were increasing, and their influence in the community was astonishing. The guilt came because of the judgment of others and comments of how the couple didn't deserve to be where they were. They were accused of being self-centered, egotistical, and entitled. Their guilt was crushing.

Another is a story of the leader of a group that disciples teenagers. The group was having a fantastic year of many teens coming to Christ through one of their programs. Their efforts were deemed as a cultish atmosphere, one that was brainwashing the teens to believe in God.

A powerful woman of God, the group's leader was devastated when one of the teen girl's father disciplined her for "falling prey to this type of belief." The judgment of the father was too much for this tenderhearted believer in Christ. She doubted her work.

When we use God's gifts to glorify Him, others will judge. God's power is most evident in us when we are weak. Remember who we are accountable to. We have to be faithful with what God has given us.

Everything we have comes from God. Our thoughts are foolish when we envy the gifts we don't receive. Enjoy the gifts God has given to others—the excitement when a friend realizes a good gift from God and the abundance that comes with it should be a natural feeling. Look upward—to heaven and to Him. Thinking less about ourselves develops the essence of humility. Not less of our worth, but less focus on our desires. It's not about us. It's all about Him.

The player knew his athletic abilities were a gift from God. He was aware that not using those gifts to the fullest was dishonoring to God. Using his platform to glorify God wasn't reliant upon the acceptance of others. It was in obeying God that he used them to represent the gospel. His wife knew she was the support God had given her husband. She knew she was to live her life with the intention to support and love her husband through this season of his life. Her gifts were no less important or powerful than his. Both were gifts from God.

The leader of the teenagers knew no man would stop the work of God. He had enabled her to speak a language that teens understood. She was able to live on a level they respected and trusted. God used her as a willing vessel to present the gospel. All given by Him. For His glory.

God loves us so much. We do not deserve the type of love He shows us. Jesus made a way to Him by dying a death for our sins and rising from the dead for life everlasting. He lives in us. We are free from an endless quest for validation in this world. We have His validation as children of an almighty God.

As believers in an almighty God, we are filled with His spirit. With His Spirit in our souls, we have the same power to love and live for the glory of God. And being beloved by Him, we pour out His love. Being servants of Christ is being Christlike. Jesus came to serve and be the ransom for many. The Bible has multiple examples of how Christ served. He served by healing lepers, washing the feet of His disciples, and talking with the woman at the well. Finishing with the greatest service of all, He served with the ultimate sacrifice of His life.

Today is our only guarantee. The only life God has given us. We let it slip past us as we fill our hands and days with busyness, distractions, regret, fear, and discontent. This life isn't practice. It is game time. We need to live it now, not tiptoe around it, not wait for the time to be just right. If we don't take risks, we end up missing the life God has given us. We miss the chance to let Him pour into us more than we could dream or imagine into and through us.

Even a whisper from God becomes the power in our lives to do anything He leads us to. What are God's dreams for us? What does He imagine for us? We won't know unless we give Him all of us, today, where we are, just as we are. Leap onto the path He has nudged you toward, or take baby steps in faith, knowing that God will do the accomplishing in and through you, and He will bring you to where He wants you to go!

*Only those who will risk going too far can possibly find out how far one can go. —T. S. Eliot*

As the book comes to an end, my journey is not complete. Neither is yours. We have a life to live and a God to glorify. God has a bigger plan for us than we could ever imagine, even when we cannot see it on the surface. He is working a miracle in us so He can be glorified through us. A divine assignment where we are positioned by God.

I know this will shock you, but I have put together a list for you. I like to have something tangible as a reminder of what I have learned, and this is something I have taped to the wall by my desk (the list moves with me when I move to a new desk in a new city).

## CRAFT YOUR LIFE EVERY DAY SO GOD CAN SAY, "WELL DONE!"

- Pray. Get alone with Jesus!
- Dig deeper into God's Word. Know Him.
- Cling to godly choices. Keep out the soul clutter. Embrace the Holy Spirit
- What can I do for others today? Find one moment. A daily touch.
- Step out in faith. Seize the moment!
- Gather! Join with others in creating this story of a life well done.

That, my friends, is a life lived well, one we will never be able to attain without His power at work in us. But we do have the ability to craft our lives for our final meeting with Jesus. The meeting that fulfills what God has done in and through us with a resounding: "Well done! Welcome home!"

# SMALL GROUP DISCUSSION GUIDE

## CHAPTER 1

1. What is God doing in and through you?
2. What is hindering you from a deeper connection to Christ?
3. Read Ephesians 3:14–21.
4. Write a dream or goal you feel God has placed on your heart. What could that dream or goal be if you allowed God to do immeasurably more in and through you according to His power?
5. How is your heart problem interfering with your spiritual life? How has God convicted you to make room for Him?

## CHAPTER 2

1. When have you felt separated from God?
2. What big rocks do you have filling the crevices of your spirit that are invading the spaces where the Holy Spirit should be roaming?
3. List the internal and external distractions you see in your life. (Yes, I know I have a problem with lists, but this will give you a visual of things to be aware of that are blocking your connection to Jesus.)
4. Read Luke 10:38–42.
   • Who do you identify with more—Martha or Mary?
   • How would you react if thirteen people showed up in your house unexpectedly?
   • What clutters your mind with worry?
   • What are some tangible ways you can stay present in His presence?
5. How did the evaluation of your heart help you in identifying the things that distract you from growing deeper with Christ?

## CHAPTER 3

1. When have you experienced a spiritual attack while serving God? Where do you see the Spirit of God working during spiritual attacks?

2. Read Matthew 3:13–17 and 4:1–11. How does this story help your awareness of spiritual attack and the guidance for the spiritual journey in life? How does it shape what it means in your life to make a difference for Christ?

3. When have you questioned God with "if You can"? What unbelief in your life can you admit and ask God to help you overcome?

4. What hurts, hang-ups, and hardships do you need to power wash from your spirit to make room for the Holy Spirit?

5. Name three people you can reach out to for help through this spiritual journey.

## CHAPTER 4

1. On a scale of 1 to 10 (least to most), rate your awareness of God in your life.

2. How is Jesus truly the Savior in your life?

3. You are God's beloved! Where do you feel this awareness the most in your life? What stops you from submitting to God's power?

4. Read Acts 6. Spirit-filled people live into the purposes of God. What story are you living now—one of a victim or a spirit-filled victor?

5. What are some ways you can increase your awareness of God and embrace the Holy Spirit in your life?

## CHAPTER 5

1. What is an experience you've had when you've listened to people rather than God? How did this experience steer you away from God's desires?

2. Describe a time when you have felt His presence in a deep and profound way.

3. Read Ephesians 5:19–20. Begin a grateful journal. Each night for a week, list (I know!) five things you are grateful for. On Sunday night, read back over the week's list. Consider making this an ongoing project. How has your heart become more thankful?

4. How does knowing God's revealed will help with not knowing His unrevealed will?

5. How is your relationship with Christ deepening? How is He working in you through this journey?

## CHAPTER 6

1. How do you hear God's guidance in your life? Can you hear Him? If not, don't let it stop you from listening.

2. When has fear of what He may say stop you from listening or asking for His guidance?

3. How can you continue to connect deeper with Christ to listen for His guidance?

4. Read 1 Samuel 3. Have you said, "Speak, Lord, for Your servant is listening"? What did you hear?

5. Who is your prayer partner? Begin to pray for someone to come into partnership with you to pray. If you have gathered people to walk this journey with you, divide into groups of two to four to pray together weekly.

## CHAPTER 7

1. How does your behavior reflect your belief? What changes do you need to make to begin to live a life on purpose?

2. What gospel influence do you have where you work, live, and play?

3. How or when has your heart been broken for the things that break God's heart?

4. Read Luke 1:26–38. How can you begin to live a whatever life?

5. What is the next one thing God is asking you to do for Him?

## CHAPTER 8

1. What is your burning desire to serve in a grand way? Is God guiding you in a different direction? How have you heard His guidance?
2. How would you describe the platform God has given you? Where are you now and how can you allow God to work through you there?
3. How can you continue to fight the good fight of faith?
4. Where are you linking arms with others? Where else can you link arms?
5. Read John 4. How is God using you in everyday life, just as you are? How can your testimony help others?

## CHAPTER 9

1. How are you living each day in response to the sacrifice Jesus made on the Cross?
2. What unique talent or gift has God given you to live on mission? Ask those you are experiencing this journey with to help you identify your talents and gifts that God can use to work through you.
3. Which doors has God closed that you are still clinging to? Which doors has He opened that you are reluctant to enter?
4. Read Mark 2:5–12. What challenges, twists, and turns are you willing to conquer to bridge the gap for someone?
5. Where do feel God drawing you to live on mission?

## CHAPTER 10

1. How has your spiritual life changed during this journey?
2. What do you want your legacy to be?
3. Read John 6:1–14. How are you seeing the crowd? What do you need to change to see the crowd clearer?
4. Do you see the life He wants you to live? How are you taking that next step of faith to live it?
5. How are you allowing God to write your story and help you craft your life to hear a resounding, "Well done!" when you meet Him face-to-face?

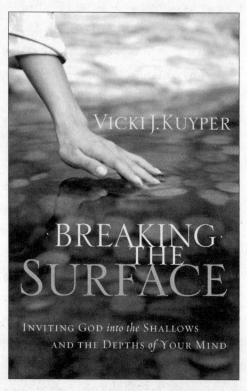

## IF YOU ENJOYED THIS BOOK, WILL YOU CONSIDER SHARING THE MESSAGE WITH OTHERS?

Let us know your thoughts at info@newhopepublishers.com. You can also let the author know by visiting or sharing a photo of the cover on our social media pages, or leaving a review at a retailer's site. All of it helps us get the message out!

Twitter.com/NewHopeBooks
Facebook.com/NewHopePublishers
Instagram.com/NewHopePublishers

---

New Hope® Publishers is a division of Iron Stream Media, which derives its name from Proverbs 27:17, "As iron sharpens iron, so one person sharpens another."

This sharpening describes the process of discipleship, one to another. With this in mind, Iron Stream Media provides a variety of solutions for churches, missionaries, and nonprofits ranging from in-depth Bible study curriculum and Christian book publishing to custom publishing and consultative services. Through the popular Life Bible Study and Student Life Bible Study brands, ISM provides web-based full-year and short-term Bible study teaching plans as well as printed devotionals, Bibles, and discipleship curriculum.

For more information on ISM and New Hope Publishers, please visit
IronStreamMedia.com
NewHopePublishers.com